24
Woodturning Projects

24
Woodturning Projects
Percy W. Blandford

TAB BOOKS

Blue Ridge Summit, PA

FIRST EDITION
FIRST PRINTING

Copyright © 1990 by TAB BOOKS
Printed in the United States of America

Library of Congress Cataloging-in-Publication Data

Blandford, Percy W.
24 woodturning projects / by Percy W. Blandford.
        p.   cm.
ISBN 0-8306-8334-8   ISBN 0-8306-3334-0 (pbk.)
1. Turning   I. Title.   II. Title: Twenty-four woodturning
                    projects.
TT201.B56   1990
684'.083—dc20   89-20655
                                                          CIP

TAB BOOKS offers software for
sale. For information and a catalog,
please contact TAB Software Department,
Blue Ridge Summit, PA 17294-0850.

Questions regarding the content of this book
should be addressed to:

Reader Inquiry Branch
TAB BOOKS
Blue Ridge Summit, PA 17294-0214

Acquisitions Editor: Kimberly Tabor
Book Editor: Steve Moro
Production: Katherine Brown

Contents

Introduction

Wood has been turned since earliest times, and often primitive lathes produced surprisingly good results. In more recent years there has been a great upsurge of interest in woodturning, and the production of more sophisticated lathes has paralleled this interest. The use of individual electric motors instead of foot power or a line shaft from a central source of power has made a modern lathe a more versatile machine tool. And it is a tool! Unlike many other machines, a lathe is a tool to be manipulated almost in the same way as hand tools, to exercise your skill. This is just one of the attractions of woodturning.

It does not take long to master the basics of woodturning, and you soon will be able to make satisfactory simple round objects. However, you have much to learn and can always increase your skill and progress to more advanced work. It is always possible, no matter how long your experience, to become a better turner. Unlike the use of some other machines, you do not have to buy expensive gadgets and extra equipment to do advanced work. It is your increasing skill with the same lathe and tools that accounts for the better and more intricate work.

With your increase in skill will come speed. You might surprise yourself with how quickly you will be able to make something that involved slow and careful tool handling when you were starting.

A problem for the enthusiastic woodturner is what to make next—and that is what this book is all about. This is an idea book. With the variations on nearly every project, there are far more ideas than the "24" indicated in the title. You only need to use a little imagination to think of more variations. Nearly all the projects described are almost entirely lathework, so you will not have to do much work away from the lathe. But if your woodworking interests expand into cabinetmaking or other bench woodwork, the ideas here can complement other things you make.

The projects in this book offer a selection from simple to advanced and from those only possible on a large lathe down to some also suitable for the smallest and simplest lathe. Most projects, however, are suitable for a lathe of the commonly used size; one that takes up to about 30 inches between centers and is able to swing 9 inches over the bed or more at the outboard end.

A woodturner can make worthwhile things from pieces of wood that other woodworkers would regard as scrap. Parts of a tree unsuitable for anything else may offer the grain pattern that is just what is needed as a feature in a turning. Some of the simplest things described in this book will be enhanced when made from wood with interesting grain.

The work of a competent turner is always in demand. Your family and friends will welcome many of the things you make from designs in this book. Besides the satisfaction you will get from turning something good you will have the added pleasure of knowing someone else will treasure your product.

That may bring you ideas of selling what you make. Woodturning is certainly an activity from which you can make a full- or part-time income. There is always a demand for individually produced turnings, such as those in this book. You may decide to tackle short runs, but do not try to compete with mass production. It is the uniqueness of your product as an individual craftsman that should appear to a customer.

You are unlikely to start with the first project and work your way through the book, but if you do, you will have an interesting time and be a better craftsman at the end! You will be more likely to dip into the book and select projects that appeal to you, or for which you have a need or some wood crying out to be used. In any case, I hope you find the appeal of turning things in wood as great as I do.

If you need more than ideas for things to make, but want some instruction in the techniques of woodturning, I suggest you purchase another of my books, *The Woodturners Bible—3rd. Edition* (TAB book #3404).

NOTE—SIZES

All sizes on drawings and in materials lists are in inches unless otherwise indicated. In most cases, widths and thicknesses are finished sizes, but lengths might be full to allow for mounting in the lathe. Where diameters are given in materials lists, these are the maximum size that will have to be turned.

1

Line Winders

If you use ropes or cord in long lengths, you should have something to wind them on if they are to be prevented from tangling or becoming untidy. This applies whether you are using lines for fishing, flying kites, keeping garden rows straight or using thicker cord for other purposes. The alternative to a reel is a flat frame, preferably with some means of turning it to wind on the line. Two examples are suggested (Fig. 1-1). The compact winder is intended for any line, and it should be suitable for holding quite long pieces in any sizes up to about $1/4$ inch in diameter. The other winder is intended for garden line. The cord is attached to the single spike, then, it is wound to the required length, and the frame spike pushed into the ground. The point under the frame also pushes into the ground and prevents the line unwinding further. When you have finished using the line, use the handle on top to rewind it.

The long spikes for the garden line winder should be steel rod $3/8$ inch in diameter, but all other parts are hardwood. The sizes shown (Fig. 1-2A) will suit the suggested uses, but they could be modified if you have special needs, without altering the method of construction. All wood parts are turned. The crossbars (Fig. 1-2B) are semicircular in section and made by dividing a turning. The main parts of both winders are made the same way, but the compact winder is described first.

Make the two crossbars by turning a solid piece and dividing it with a fine saw. Another way is to start with two pieces glued together with paper between (Fig. 1-3A). After turning, split along the paper line with a knife or chisel and sand off the excess paper. Turn a cylinder with rounded ends (Fig. 1-3B). It will help in locating holes, as well as provide decoration, if lines are cut round at the main hole positions. Burn them in if you wish.

Drill $3/8$-inch holes across for the rungs (Fig. 1-2C and D). The axle could be thicker, depending on the strength of wood, but $7/16$ inch or $1/2$ inch should do. Do not drill the end hole (Fig. 1-3C) for this winder.

Turn the two rungs (Fig. 1-3D), with the ends reduced to fit in the crossbar holes. Use hardwood dowel rod, or turn the rungs from square stock.

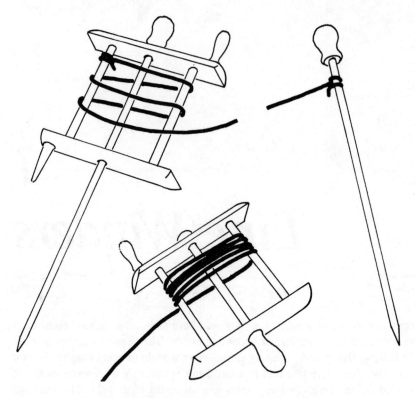

Fig. 1-1. A line winder may hold a garden line or cord for other purposes.

Materials List for Line Winders

Compact Line Winder

2 crossbars	$9 \times 1^{1}/_{4} \times {}^{5}/_{8}$
2 rungs	$6 \times {}^{1}/_{2}$ diameter
1 axle	$8 \times {}^{7}/_{16}$ diameter
1 handle	$4 \times {}^{3}/_{4}$ diameter
1 handle	3×1 diameter

Garden Line Winder

2 crossbars	$9 \times 1^{1}/_{4} \times {}^{5}/_{8}$
2 rungs	$6 \times {}^{1}/_{2}$ diameter
2 knobs	$2 \times 1^{1}/_{4}$ diameter
1 handle	$4 \times {}^{3}/_{4}$ diameter
1 point	$4 \times {}^{3}/_{4}$ diameter
2 spikes	$18 \times {}^{3}/_{8}$ diameter steel rod

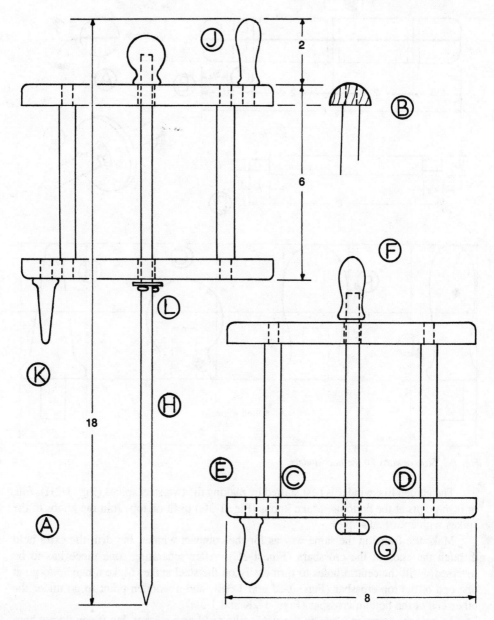

Fig. 1-2. Suggested sizes for line winders.

Separate the two crossbars and drill one end hole (Fig. 1-2E). Turn a handle to fit that hole (Fig. 1-3E). Glue together the rungs, crossbar and handle.

Turn an axle or choose a piece of dowel rod to slide easily through the center holes. Turn a slightly thicker handle to fit on its end (Figs. 1-2F and 1-3F). Make a small button (Fig. 1-2G), like a wooden washer, to glue on the end of the axle. Assemble these parts so the frame turns easily on the axle.

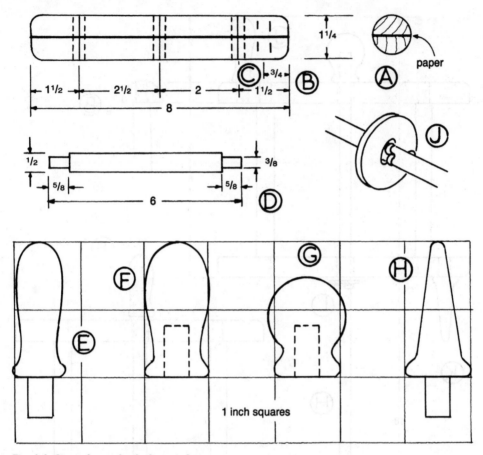

Fig. 1-3. Sizes of parts for the line winders.

The garden line winder is best started by making the two steel spikes (Fig. 1-2H). File or turn points at the bottoms. Make knobs (Fig. 1-3G) to fit on top. Join the knobs to the spikes with epoxy adhesive.

Make the frame in the same way as for the compact winder, but drill the extra hold through the ends of the crossbars (Fig. 1-3C). After separating, one piece has to be reversed. Drill the central holes to turn easily on the steel spike. Make a handle to go at one end of the top crossbar (Figs. 1-2J and 1-3E), and a wooden point to go under the other end of the bottom crossbar (Figs. 1-2K and 1-3H).

To hold the frame in place on the steel spike weld on a washer, but if you do not have welding facilities, drill across for a split cotter pin (Figs. 1-2L and 1-3J).

Both winders could be used without treatment, but it would be better to seal and protect the wood with paint or varnish. A bright color will help you find your winder in grass or on a garden.

2

Towel and Curtain Rails

Towels and curtain or drapes present similar problems of hanging—the difference is mainly in scale. In both cases, most or all parts can be made on a lathe. There are rails and rings with brackets of various types for mounting on a wall. Although some rails might be softwood, use hardwood for brackets, pedestals, and rings. For a natural finish in a bathroom or kitchen light-colored wood looks most hygienic.

Towels may be hung from pegs, rings, or rails. Sizes and quantity of towels will determine what you make. The simplest item is a single peg (Figs. 2-1A and 2-2A). This has the advantage of fitting almost any restricted space, if necessary. It may be all you need for a hand towel or drying cloth, and it can double as a place to hang a coat or apron.

The peg (Fig. 2-2B) has a dowel end to fit into a hole, a shoulder next to it and a reduced parallel spindle for the towel, finishing with a knob to prevent the towel falling off. If you make the peg before the back plate, drill a 3/4-inch hole in a piece of scrap wood for testing the dowel size.

The back plate (Fig. 2-2C) is a disc with a molded edge. Several moldings are possible, but the simple one shown is appropriate to the design. Use two screw holes on opposite sides, but three equally spaced also look good. Screws could be countersunk, but round head plated screws provide a neat finish.

One way of turning the disc back plate is to use a screw center while cutting the shape; then, start the central hole with a suitable drill mounted in a chuck in the tailstock, before removing the wood from the lathe and drilling right through on the bench or in a drill press.

Save yourself the trouble of planing the dowel level after assembly by turning the dowel end short (Fig. 2-2D) in this and similar assemblies.

To hang more than one towel, make a series of similar pegs and mount them on a long strip of wood.

Supports for a rail for a towel or narrow curtain can be made in a very similar way to

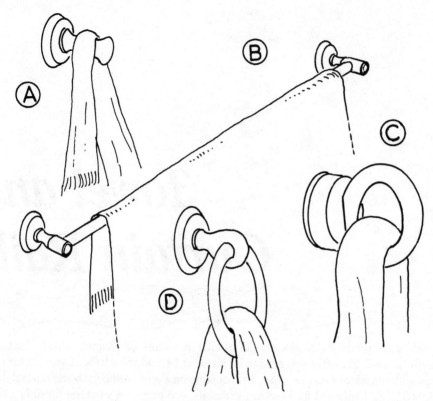

Fig. 2-1. Turned pegs, rails and rings for hanging towels.

the first example (Figs. 2-1B and 2-2E). The back plate is the same, but the screw holes should be arranged to when you need to use a screwdriver it will be clear of the rail.

To allow sufficient wood for strength after drilling, the outer part of the peg is cylindrical (Fig. 2-2F) and turned with a dowel end. The distance from the wall shown should suit most needs, but make the peg any length.

Turn the rail or use a piece of $5/8$-inch or $3/4$-inch dowel rod. Plated metal tube would be an attractive alternative. Drill the pegs to a little further than halfway through.

A towel might be hung by passing through a rigid ring (Figs. 2-1C and 2-3A), but as this will project several inches from the wall, do not position it where it could be knocked and damaged.

The back plate for this hanger could be the same as for the first two examples, but without the dowel hole. The ring might be turned with a round cross-section, or form the section rectangular with rounded corners. Also, it might be octagonal. Choose wood with close grain for the ring. A piece with confused twisted grain might make a stronger ring than one with a straight grain.

Plane off the ring in the direction of the grain to fit against the back plate (Fig. 2-3B). Take off a sufficient amount to provide space for two screws. Drill the back plate for the two flat-head screws, and mark through for tapping holes in the ring. Be careful to get the ring central and upright. Use glue as well as screws in the final assembly. Drill for two screws to the wall.

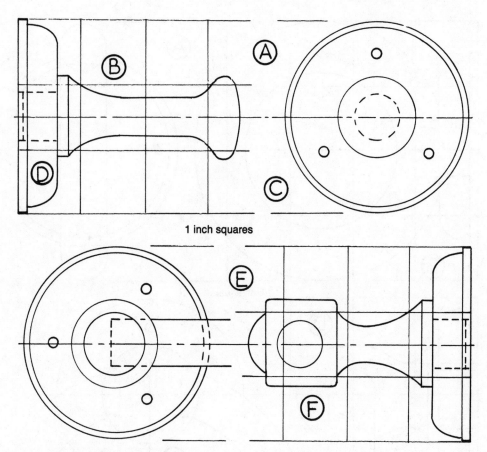

1 inch squares

Fig. 2-2. Sizes for towel pegs and rail.

A swinging ring towel holder (Fig. 2-1D) is more usual. The suggested size has a ring 5 inches in diameter (Fig. 2-3C), made in a similar way to the rigid ring, but with a round cross-section. Turn a full circle, and cut the gap later.

Make a back plate similar to the earlier examples and with a $3/4$-inch hole. The peg need not project very far. It could be made like the one for holding a rail (Fig. 2-2F), but it is shown oval in the side view (Fig. 2-3D).

Drill in opposite sides of the peg to take the ring ends. The holes will probably be $3/4$ inch in diameter, but check the ring section size. The ring ends will have to be sprung in, so do not make the holes very deep—$1/4$-inch will probably be enough.

Make the cut in the ring in the side grain, which will be the strongest way. Make the gap the same as the distance between the bottoms of the holes. You will probably have to ease the cut ends of the ring a little by sanding, so they will spring into the holes and allow a limited swing.

You might find it simpler for this and the fixed ring towel holder to apply the chosen finish before final assembly.

Supports for curtain or drape rails or rods can be made in the same way as towel rail supports if the rail is not very thick or long. However, if it is thicker and has to be held

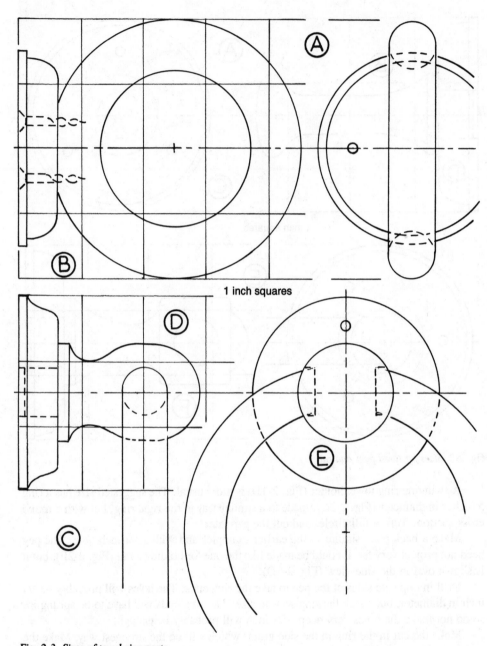

1 inch squares

Fig. 2-3. Sizes of towel ring parts.

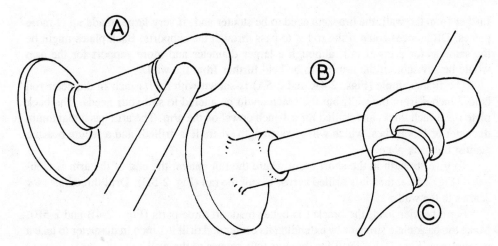

Fig. 2-4. Two types of curtain rail supports.

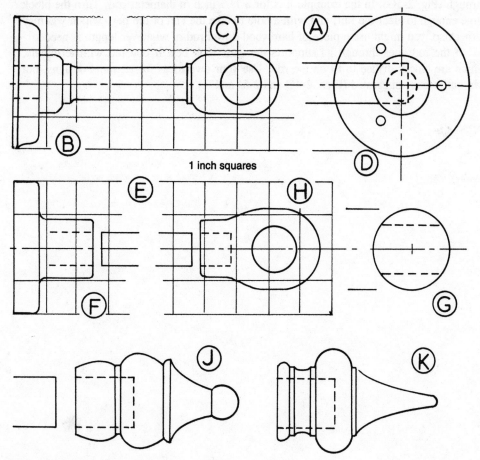

1 inch squares

Fig. 2-5. Sizes and patterns for curtain rail supports.

further from the wall, the brackets need to be stouter and, if very large, made up of more pieces. Differences come if the rod is to pass through the supports. Back plates might be the same as for a towel rail, although a larger diameter and more support for the arm would be advisable if the rail has to be held further from the wall.

The first example (Figs. 2-4A and 2-5A) is shown with a $1^1/_4$-inch in diameter rod held 7 inches from the wall, but the reach could be altered to suit your needs. The back plate is $^3/_4$-inch thick, and drilled for a 1-inch dowel on the arm. The arm has a maximum diameter of $1^3/_4$ inches, which will give strength where it is drilled, and a secure bearing against the back plate.

To give strength in the short grain where the rail enters, the end of the arm is elongated (Fig. 2-5C), then it is drilled across to suit the rail (Fig. 2-5D). Drill three holes for screws to the wall.

For a heavier load, the bracket is better made in three parts (Figs. 2-4B and 2-5E). Make the back plate stronger by extending its center and drill it 1 inch in diameter to take a parallel peg (Fig. 2-5F). Drill for three or four screws to the wall.

Larger rails are usually taken through their supports, so you need to allow for a hole through (Fig. 2-5G). In the example it is for a $1^1/_2$ inch in diameter rod. Turn the block large enough to clear the rail, and with a hole to take the end of the peg. which you may turn. Also, you might use a piece of hardwood dowel rod of whatever length is needed.

If the rod goes through its supports the ends look best if covered with terminals, which are blocks drilled to fit on the rod. Use your own ideas for terminal designs, but two outlines are suggested (Figs. 2-4C and 2-5J and K).

3
Candlesticks

Over the centuries, some of the most attractive products of the lathe have been candlesticks in a multitude of different forms. Wood does not often endure for long periods, but there are brass candlesticks in churches and cathedrals that show their origin a great many years ago as they were cast from wooden originals. In many cases, the wooden candlestick would have been just as servicable, if not as durable, as the brass version made from it. These candlesticks provide examples of design which would still be worth following.

Candles are no longer an essential of life, but candlesticks are still sought after for their decorative value and for use as table centers on special occasions. The fashion for ornamental candles has brought a revival of interest in things to hold them, and this is an opportunity for the turner.

When planning a candlestick design, it should be related to its use. If it is only expected to be decorative in itself with possibly an occasional use with a plain candle, the design is self-contained. If a very ornate candle is to be used with it, the woodwork may be supplementary to the candle and the total effect would benefit by having the woodwork fairly plain.

In its simplest form, the central column is turned with the socket in the same piece of wood (Fig. 3-1A). The hole in the end should suit the chosen size of the candle. It will be between 3/4 inch and 1 inch for standard candles, but it is advisable to check on locally available candles before starting work.

Make a plug to represent the end of the candle. Let this be a little longer than the socket to be drilled and retain its center hollow (Fig. 3-1B). Rough-turn the piece of wood that is to form the column, then, drill the hole for the candle using a drill in a tailstock chuck (Fig. 3-1C). Push the plug into this hole and do the rest of the turning with the plug in place (Fig. 3-1D).

Further turning is straightforward. Drill a hole in a piece of scrap wood and use this to check the dowel end of the column, either directly or by using it as a guide to caliper setting. Turn the base to match on a faceplate.

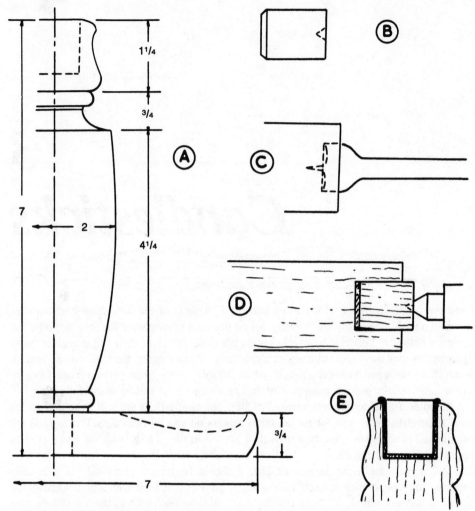

Fig. 3-1. Steps in making a wooden candlestick.

Metal candle sockets can be bought to fit in the top of the column (Fig. 3-1E). If one of these is used, that will settle the size hole to drill. A metal socket makes a neat mount for the candle, but check first that it matches available candles.

There are many developments on this basic candlestick. If serious use is intended, there should be a drip ring to catch candle grease. This improves the appearance of the candlestick in any case, even if candles will rarely be lit. A good way to include this is to let the actual candleholder and the drip ring fit over a dowel end on the column (Fig. 3-2A). Both parts are drilled to a size to suit the candle and the top of the column turned to fit.

The candleholder has its grain lengthwise. If a self-centering chuck is available, the blank can be held in this to drill through. Otherwise, an overlength piece can be made cylindrical between centers, then drilled from the tailstock (Fig. 3-2B). The outside can

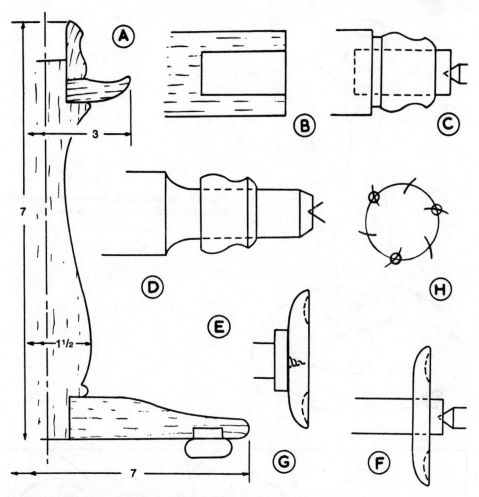

Fig. 3-2. Details of a candlestick with feet and a drip ring.

be finished with a plug in the hole (Fig. 3-2C). Alternatively the blank can be mounted on a mandrel (Fit. 3-2D).

If the drip ring is not very large, it might also have its grain parallel with the hole, but for most sizes, it will have to be turned from a disc with its grain across. It might be possible to turn it on a screw center so the flat part can come on the underside (Fig. 3-2E). The hole is drilled after turning has been completed. The screw hole will center the drill accurately. This could leave too large an area of flat for some purposes. It might be better then to do all of the turning with the ring mounted on a mandrel (Fig. 3-2F).

A flat surface on the bottom might be satisfactory as most candlesticks stand on level surfaces. Cover the bottom with cloth or one of the self-adhesive clothlike plastics. Alternatively, turn the bottom hollow so it rests on the rim. A way of ensuring standing level, whatever the surface, is to arrange the weight to be taken on three feet, which will rest without wobbling no matter how uneven the surface. The feet can be turned with dowels to

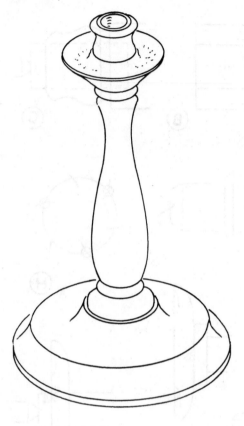

Fig. 3-3. The candlestick shown is made from four parts: base, spindle, drip ring, and candleholder.

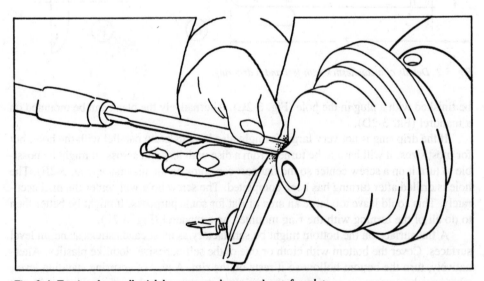

Fig. 3-4. Turning the candlestick base mounted on a pad or a faceplate.

fit into holes in the base (Fig. 3-2G). To get an even pitch circle, draw a circle of the desired size and step off the radius around it. As the radius goes exactly six times, the dowel holes are at alternate points (Fig. 3-2H).

The steps involved in making a similar candlestick (Fig. 3-3) are shown in the photographs. The base is turned on a faceplate (Fig. 3-4), and the hole for the dowel on the stem is drilled from the tailstock. The stem is turned between centers. On it, the dowel that will pass through the drip ring and candleholder can be checked for size with a hole in a scrap piece of wood when the tailstock is withdrawn, but the dowel that has to fit in the base must be tested with calipers (Fig. 3-5). The candleholder is a simple exercise in outside turning on an arbor (Fig. 3-6). The drip ring is made from a disc with its grain across and has to be turned carefully on both sides (Fig. 3-7).

A candlestick does not have to be tall. For the decorative candles that are individually made, it is better for the holder to be little more than a block of wood with a hole in it (Fig. 3-8A). Anyone with a lathe will want to do something more than just have a plain block, but excessive turning detail should be avoided, and the finished work should have a broad base if the candle is very large (Fig. 3-8B). Blocks could be built up with different colored woods.

This is an opportunity to use up scrap wood too small to be built into anything large. In some cases, it may be advisable to join two pieces so the actual holder is mounted on (Fig. 3-8E). Single-block stands can be made to suit the small candles used as Christmas decorations, but the bottom should be broad and heavy (Fig. 3-8F). A lit candle, of any size, could be dangerous if knocked over.

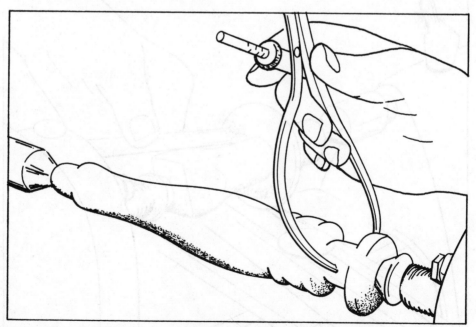

Fig. 3-5. The pedestal has been turned, and the dowel to fit the base is checked for size.

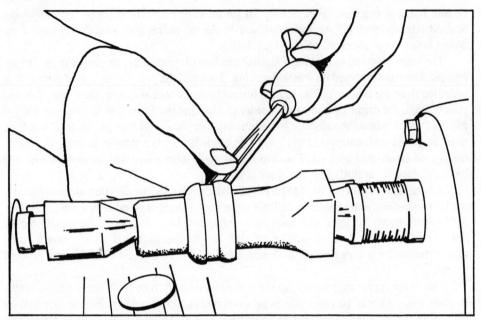

Fig. 3-6. The candleholder is made from a drilled block mounted on an arbor.

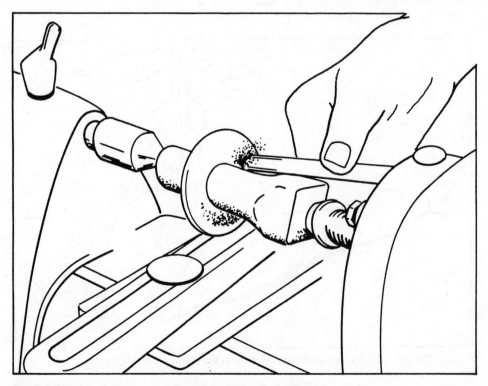

Fig. 3-7. The drip ring on an arbor has to be turned on both sides.

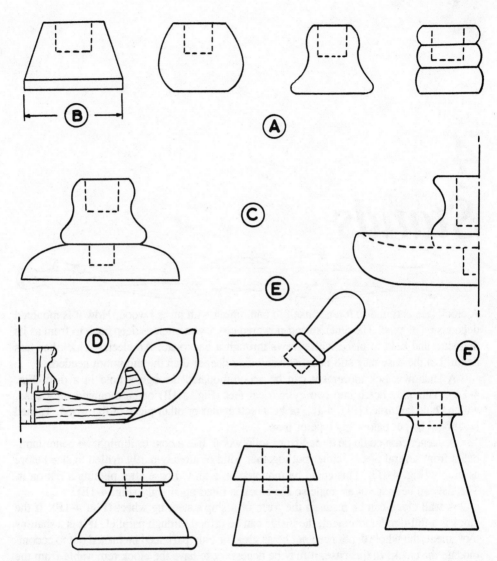

Fig. 3-8. Some examples of small candlesticks.

another piece forming a base (Fig. 3-8C). This could be developed further and the base turned up like a bowl to hold small items and look like the candlestick that people used to light before the days of electricity. To complete the illusion, there could be a handle let into the rim (Fig. 3-8D). Another treatment would be a turned handle doweled into the base

4
Stands

A clock face is round so it lends itself to combining with turned wood. How it is mounted depends on its type. The older spring-powered clock was often as deep back to front as its diameter and held in place with screws through a backplate. An electric clock has less depth, but the case may still benefit from being deeper than the minimum needed.

A shallow clock movement can be accommodated through a hole in a disc (Fig. 4-1A). This may notch into two cylindrical feet (Fig. 4-1B) or be mounted on a base, which could be turned (Fig. 4-1C) or be a rectangular or other piece of flat wood. Turned feet could be put below any type of base.

A deeper case could be turned from solid wood, like a box, or it might be better laminated from several pieces, either put together solid or already partly drilled to size before assembly (Fig. 4-1D). This could be mounted on a turned base after planing a flat on it. The flat can be made at an angle so the clock is tilted up slightly (Fig. 4-1E).

A wall clock can be made in the form of a ship's steering wheel (Fig. 4-1F). If the clock is a full-depth movement, the inside can be turned through parallel. If it is a shallow movement, the whole depth need not be as great or only part need be turned out to accommodate the clock. In this case, it may be necessary to have the clock removable from the front if it needs attention, or a small diameter hole taken through to the back to give access.

The main problem with a ship's wheel design is in getting the handles positioned truly, because slight errors will be very obvious. The number of handles depends on the size of the whole thing. Six or eight are a reasonable choice, and five is the minimum. Handles of a genuine ship's wheel are all identical, except one is given an extra bead or other marking. When this is at the top, the rudder is straight. In a clock, this could also be at the top.

If the lathe has a dividing head, the positions of the spokes can be marked along the tool rest with its aid. Otherwise, a strip of paper wrapped around it to get the circumference, which can be divided when the paper is flattened, is the safest way of dividing.

Run a line around the cylinder by holding a pencil against the revolving wood (Fig.

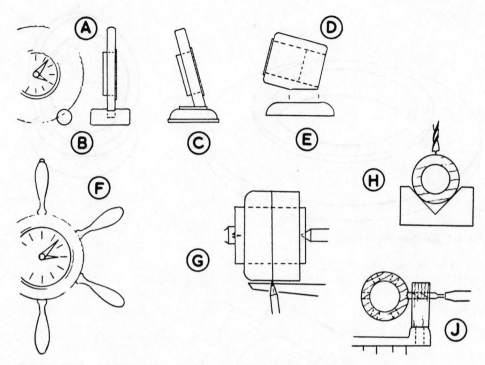

Fig. 4-1. Clocks and thermometers can be mounted in turned wooden cases.

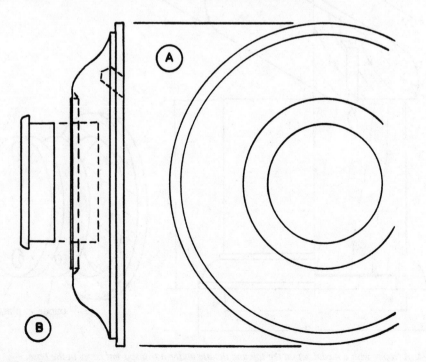

Fig. 4-2. A thermometer case to hang on the wall.

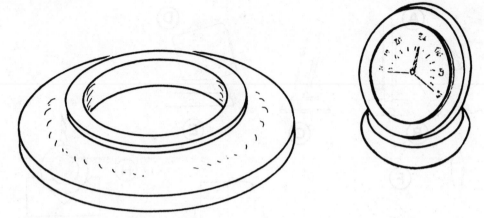

Fig. 4-3. Two thermometer stands and cases.

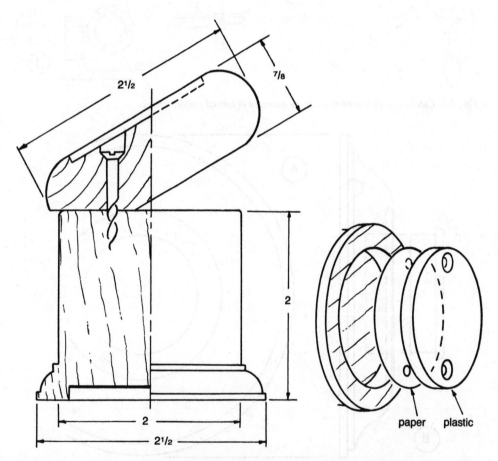

Fig. 4-4. A trophy with a medal set on the top and details under a transparent cover in the base.

4-1G). Holes for the handles can be drilled accurately if the cylinder is held truly on V-blocks, which may be improvised for the purpose (Fig. 4-1H). Another way is to mount a wood block in place of the tool rest and have a hole accurately drilled through this at center height. A hand electric drill can be used with this as a guide (Fig. 4-1J).

There are other round instruments that can be mounted in a similar way. These include thermometers, hygrometers, and barometers, all of which are shallow in relation to their diameters.

A simple mounting is little more than a hollowed disc to screw on the wall (Fig. 4-2A). The outside may be turned with a molding to give a more decorative appearance (Fig. 4-2B).

A tubular mounting can be made similar to a clock. In fact, it may be possible to make a clock and a thermometer or other instrument as a pair.

Another way to mount a round instrument is in a disc with another matching disc as a base. The case is planed with a flat for gluing and screwing that puts it at a convenient angle (Fig. 4-3) for viewing when standing on a table.

Medals and other ornamental discs are often used as trophies and gifts within clubs and organizations. After presentation, the recipient may wonder what to do with his or her award. This also applies to unusual coins. The turned design shown is intended to provide a way of mounting any round metal disc of this sort and make it into a trophy, which could

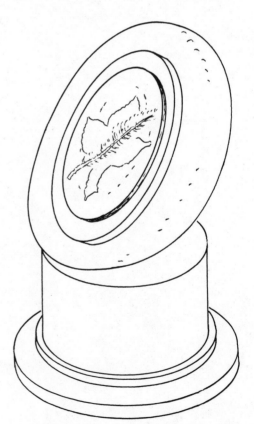

Fig. 4-5. The trophy showing the onset medal.

be used for regular competition or just a means of displaying what has already been won (Figs. 4-4 and 4-5).

The medal or coin fits into a recess in a wood disc, where it is glued, unless you want to be able to lift it out and examine the other side. Turn the disc with a rounded or molded edge on a screw center. The hole from the screw will not be very obvious underneath in the finished trophy, particularly if you fill it with stopping or drill it out for a wood plug.

The stand could be any height and is shown with parallel sides and a molded base. If the item is to be used for regular competition or you wish to keep a record of how the medal was won, there can be a paper in the base on which details may be written. Cut a circle of transparent plastic to go over the circle of paper. Turn a recess in the base deep enough for these to come just below the surface. Drill for two screws to hold the plastic and paper in, so they can be opened if a new entry has to be made.

If the trophy is to stand on a table, the top part should be at a flatter angle than if it is to go higher on a shelf. It is shown at 30 degrees to horizontal, which should suit a table position. Bevel the underside and drill for a screw. Use glue as well and also glue in the medal or coin.

5
Stools

Turned legs for tables, chairs, and other furniture are a regular type of work for a wood-turner, and these are usually made in sets of four, but other parts of the projects involve cabinetry rather than work on a lathe. Stools might also have parts made elsewhere than on a lathe, but many stool parts can be made completely on a lathe, with a round top and legs, and often round rails or stretchers.

In early days, when earth or stone floors were uneven, much use was made of three-legged stools, because the tripod arrangement of legs would always stand on any surface without wobbling. Three legs would always find a level. If you have four legs and the surface is uneven, two opposite legs will take the weight and you wobble from one to the other on the other two. Of course, in modern homes all floors should be level and four-legged stools, as well as other furniture, can be expected to stand steadily. However, three-legged stools are attractive and have advantages outdoors, where you may be away from level floors. Turned stools with three legs make interesting lathe projects.

In the days when cows were milked by hand in dirt-floored sheds or in the open, the milk maid relied on a three-legged stool to give her a steady and safe seat. You will not want one for its original purpose, but a traditional milking stool is interesting to make and your family will find many uses for it when finished.

The stool shown (Fig. 5-1A) is fairly plain, as it would have been originally, but if you want to decorate by turning beads and coves you might use your own ideas.

The sizes suggested (Fig. 5-2A) make a seat of comfortable height, which is a little more than would have been required for milking. Almost any hardwood can be used. The size of the top might have to be limited by the swing over the bed of your lathe, if it is not equipped for outboard turning. As the rigidity of the legs depend on their joints to the top, that should be thick enough to provide rigidity and 1¹/₄-inch minimum is suggested.

The top is a 10-inch disc (Fig. 5-2B) which can be turned on a faceplate, as plugged screw holes underneath will not show in the finished stool. Round the edges and cut rings round if you wish. Cut a 6 inches in diameter circle on the top surface. Besides serving as decoration, this becomes the pitch circle for the leg holes. Step off their positions.

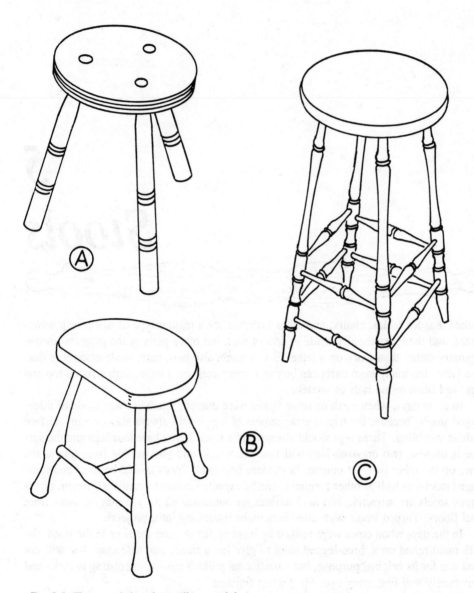

Fig. 5-1. Three stools based on milking stool designs.

Make three matching legs (Fig. 5-2C). Drill a 1-inch hole in scrap wood with the bit you will use for the top. Turn the leg tops to fit this, and finish most of the rest of the length to about 1¹/₂ inches in diameter. Round the legs' bottoms. Decorate with cut lines, which could be burned in for greater emphasis.

The legs have to be splayed so their ends are about 2-inches outside the top, when viewed from above (Fig 5-2D). The holes in the top must be drilled to suit. It is important that all legs are at the same angle, even if that is not exactly as originally planned. You might be able to tile the top on a drill press to get all three holes at the same angle. Alternatively, make a template of the intended angle to guide the drill when boring freehand (Fig. 5-2E).

Make saw cuts in the tops of the legs for wedges. Let the legs go through a short distance as you glue them in, and arrange the saw cuts across the grain of the top (Fig. 5-2F), so when you drive the wedges they do not have a splitting action. Level the tops of the legs when the glue has set.

The traditional stool would have been left untreated, but you might wish to apply a clear varnish.

The second stool (Fig. 5-1B) is also based on a milking stool, but the straight edge serves as a front and the rails strengthen the leg assembly, as well as provide decoration. As shown (Fig. 5-3A) all outlines are plain, following the prototype, which was purely functional. You could put more shape into the legs and rails, similar to the next example, or match the design of chair legs in the same room.

The top starts as a 12-inch circle with rounded edges. Mark on its underside the positions of holes for the legs. Make a straight cut parallel to two holes (Fig. 5-3B). Arrange hole positions and cut this in the direction of the grain. Round the cut corners.

The three legs are the same (Fig. 5-3C), but the rail holes are at slightly different angles. Turn the legs to fit holes in the stool top, drilled by one of the methods described for the first stool. The angle for all three legs, arranged radially, is as shown for the back leg (Fig. 5-3D). Mark a rail hole position on each leg, but do not drill the holes yet.

Turn the two rails to fit $3/4$-inch holes. The overall length of the front rail (Fig. 5-3E) is 10 inches and the other rail (Fig. 5-3F) is $8^{1}/_{2}$ inches, but allow a little extra for trimming, in case the final splay of the legs is not quite as intended. The center of each rail should be $1^{1}/_{4}$ inches in diameter. Drill the front rail to take one end of the other rail.

A trial assembly of the front legs will let you check the length of the front rail and determine the angle to drill holes in the legs for its ends. A further trial assembly allows

Materials List for Stools

First stool

3 legs	16 × 1 $^{1}/_{2}$ diameter	
1 top	10 × 10	×1$^{1}/_{4}$

Second stool

3 legs	14 × 1 $^{3}/_{4}$ diameter	
1 rail	11 × 1 $^{1}/_{4}$ diameter	
1 rail	9 × 1 $^{1}/_{4}$ diameter	
1 top	12 × 12	×1$^{1}/_{2}$

Third stool

4 legs	28 × 1 $^{1}/_{2}$ diameter	
8 rails	15 × 1 $^{1}/_{4}$ diameter	
1 top	12 × 12	×1$^{1}/_{4}$

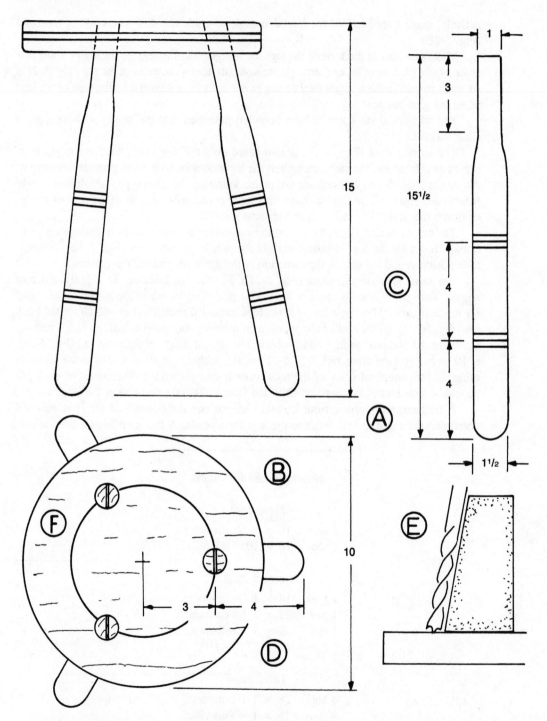

Fig. 5-2. Sizes and parts of a three-legged round stool.

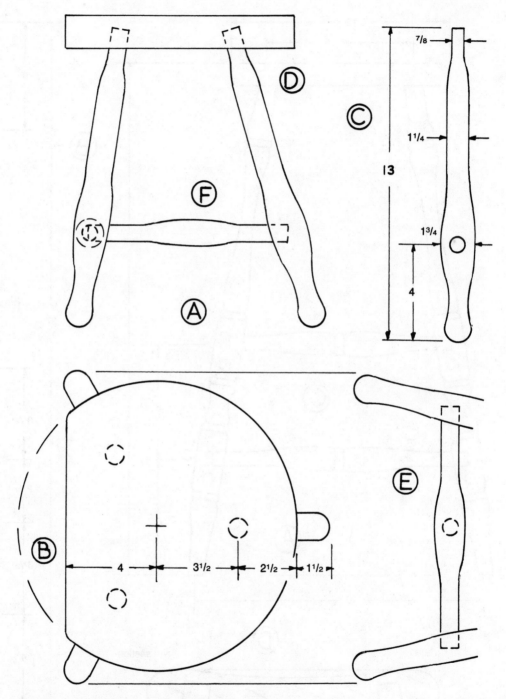

Fig. 5-3. A three-legged stool with a straight edge and rails.

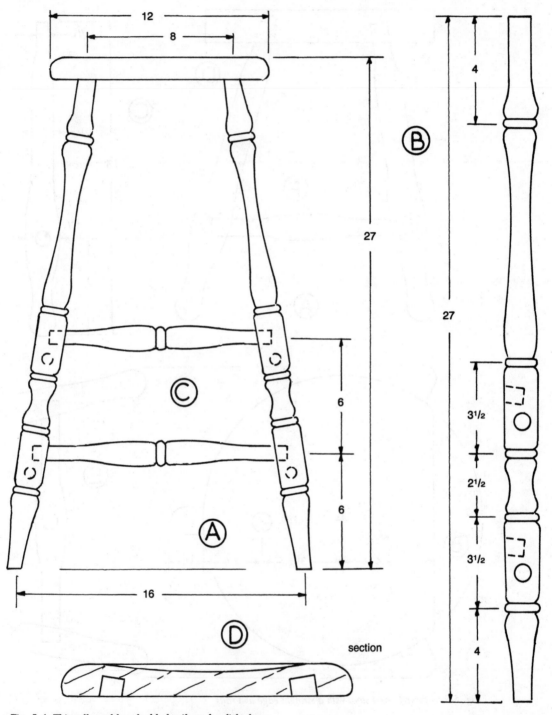

Fig. 5-4. This tall stool has doubled rails and a dished top.

you to make the same checks for the other rail and the hole in the rear leg. It should be satisfactory to drill all rail holes halfway through.

It might simplify assembly to join the two rails into a T-shape and let that glue set before gluing the legs into the top and the rails into the legs. Stain to match other furniture, or apply a clear finish.

The third stool (Fig. 5-1C) has a turned top and four legs joined by two rails each side. It is shown (Fig. 5-4) as a tall stool, but the same design could be used for a lower stool. The rails enter each leg at different levels, so they can be taken deeper to produce stronger joints than if the rails had to meet in the legs at the same level.

It will help in getting the lengths and positions of rails, as well as the angles of the holes, if you set out the main centerlines of a side view (Fig. 5-4A) fullsize.

Make the legs (Fig. 5-4B). Keep the maximum size of $1^1/_2$ inches in diameter at the cylindrical parts where the rail join. Cut beads where shown, then shape the parts between and reduce top and bottom to 1 inch in diameter. Pencil round the hole positions while the wood is still rotating in the lathe. Check that the legs match each other.

Get out the rail lengths from your setting. Make each rail $1^1/_4$ inches in diameter with a bead at the center and taper to fit $5/_8$-inch holes at the ends (Fig. 5-4C). Drill the legs to about half thickness.

Turn the top with a well-rounded upper edge and a lesser-rounded lower edge. A slight hollow in the top will improve comfort (Fig. 5-4D). Mark the intended positions of the holes for the legs on the underside.

If you make a trial assembly of the legs and rails, this will allow you to check the positions for the holes marked under the top and modify the layout if necessary. Also, it will show you the angles to drill the holes.

Assemble two opposite pairs of legs and their rails first, and see that they match as a pair. Add the rails the other way and fit the top. View the assembly from several angles to see that the stool stands upright and all legs have matching slopes. Make any adjustments before the glue starts setting.

An attractive hardwood could be given a clear finish, but the stool looks good painted, possibly with the top a different color from the lower parts.

6
Two-tier Tray

A pair of circular trays on a central pedestal with a lifting handle can have many uses. The double tray can display a collection of souvenirs. It might be piled with fruit on a side table. It could make a dining table feature, holding cakes, preserves or condiments. Whatever its contents, it may be passed around easily by using the handle.

It is possible to make such a two-tier tray any size. The example shown (Fig. 6-1) is a fairly substantial design, able to take a large amount of fruit or other weighty items. You could lighten sections, but it would be unwise to reduce the tray thicknesses much because of the risk of warping. You could increase to three trays by including another spindle section.

As drawn (Fig. 6-2) the bottom tray is 14 inches in diameter. If you cannot fit that size in your lathe you will have to modify the design. Both trays could be made from a single piece of wood, but you might join several narrow strips to make up the width; this would also help to counteract any tendency to warp. An interesting pattern could be made by joining strips which alternate in different colors. Do not use softwoods.

The half sections (Fig. 6-2A) show how the parts are assembled. There are four feet under the bottom tray; then, a pedestal fits into a central hole and into a similar hole in a pad under the top tray. So the parts will be kept in line, the dowel in the bottom spindle projects a short distance into the top tray hole (Fig. 6-2B). The handle is made with pegs into opposite sides of the knob (Fig. 6-2C).

Materials List for Two-tier Tray	
1 tray	14 × 14 × 1¹/₂
1 tray	10 × 10 × 1¹/₂
2 spindles	9 × 2 diameter
2 pegs	4 × 1 diameter
4 feet	6 × 1 diameter

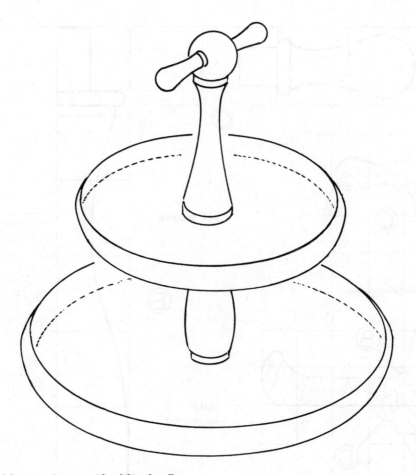

Fig. 6-1. A two-tier tray with a lifting handle.

Turn the two trays first. They have similar rims and start 1 1/2-inches thick, but are reduced so most of the section finishes 3/4-inch thick (Fig. 6-3A and B). Start with the wood planed flat to bear on a pad on the faceplate. Any screw holes underneath may be plugged later. Drill the central hole in the lathe. Make four holes for the feet dowels equally spaced under the bottom tray (Fig. 6-3C).

Turn the pad (Figs. 6-2D and 6-3D) on a screw center, and drill the central hole partially; then, finish it after removing from the lathe. An alternative is to drill the hole first and mount the wood on a mandrel for turning.

Turn the dowels on the lower part of the pedestal (Fig. 6-2E), with the top one long enough to project through the pad 1/8-inch for locating the top tray. Make the shoulders behind the dowels flat or slightly hollow, so they bed tightly in place when you assemble.

Turn the dowel on the top pedestal (Fig. 6-2F), with a flat or hollow shoulder; this dowel should not quite meet the end of the lower dowel in the hole in the top tray. Turn the knob spherical or elliptical. Mark opposite sides for the peg holes.

Make the two pegs to match each other (Fig. 6-2G). To get a close fit, flatten a little

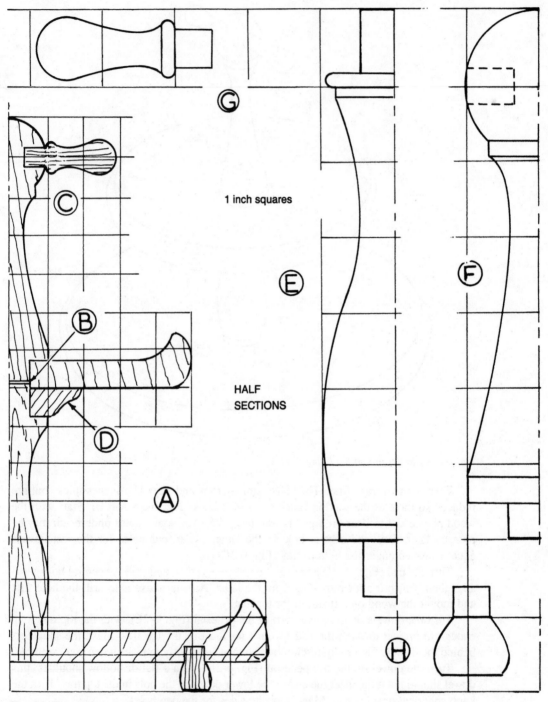

1 inch squares

HALF
SECTIONS

Fig. 6-2. Sizes and sections of parts of the two-tier tray.

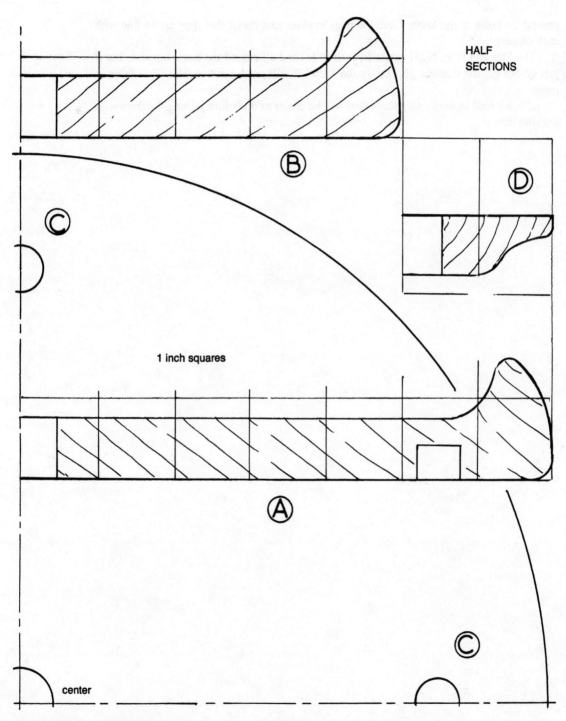

HALF
SECTIONS

B

D

C

1 inch squares

A

C

center

Fig. 6-3. Sections and layout of two trays.

around the holes in the knob. Glue the pegs in place and check that they are in line with each other.

The four feet (Fig. 6-2H) must fit their holes and all extend the same amount, but if you do not get the outlines all exactly the same, it will not be noticeable. Glue them in place.

If you intend to stain and polish, that will be easier to do before joining the trays with the spindles.

Lazy Susan Bowls

You may enjoy turning bowls, but there is a limit to the demand for simple bowls, and you could reach a stage where you are looking for further developments on the same theme on which to exercise your skill. This project is a large bowl or tray into which three other bowls fit. You could leave it at that. However, this design goes on to include a base and a ball bearing turntable, so that the large bowl and its contents can be revolved (Fig. 7-1). The three smaller bowls can be lifted out. The complete project may have many uses, particularly for offering a selection of fruit, nuts, and other foods.

Three inner bowls are chosen for geometric reasons; they can be made to fit against each other and the large bowl with the minimum waste space (Fig. 7-2A). If you fit four bowls, they will be smaller and there will be a larger gap in the middle (Fig. 7-2B). This might be a good arrangement if you want to have a lifting handle at the center. The next geometric step, where small bowls can be arranged to touch each other and fit closely, is seven (Fig. 7-2C), but that would result in rather tiny bowls, unless you made the whole assembly quite large.

For the project shown (Fig. 7-3A) sizes might be dictated by the wood available and the maximum circle you can turn on your lathe. When you know the size, draw the intended inside circle and step off the radius around the circumference (Fig. 7-2D). Join these six points. The size of a small bowl will be a circle drawn on one line to touch the adjoining lines and the large circle (Fig. 7-2E). In the project as drawn, the circle inside

Materials List for Lazy Susan Bowls		
1 bowl	14 × 14 × 2½	
1 base	14 × 14 × 1	
3 bowls	6 × 6 × 2¼	

Fig. 7-1. Three bowls contained in another which is on a revolving base.

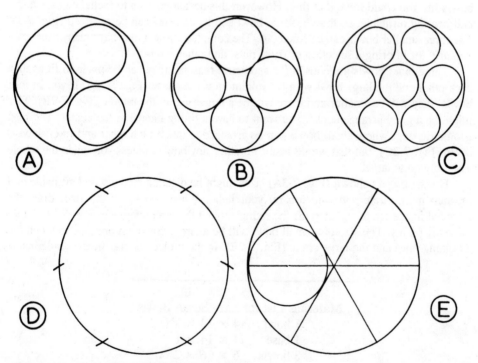

Fig. 7-2. Layout possibilities for the Lazy Susan bowls.

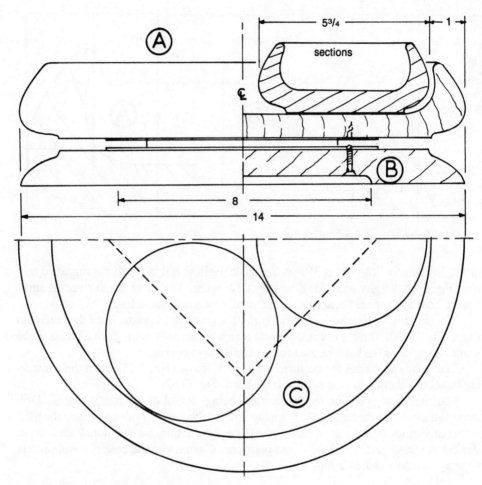

Fig. 7-3. Suggested sizes for the Lazy Susan bowls.

the large bowl is 12 inches in diameter, and a small bowl is 5³/₄ inches in diameter. Allow a little clearance. Turn the large bowl, and check its inside diameter before setting out and deciding on the size of the small bowls.

Select a good hardwood. The small bowls could be a different color wood from the large bowl and its base. If you have to glue pieces to make up width for the large parts, they could alternate in different colors.

It is possible to get several sizes of Lazy Susan bearings. As an example, a 6-inch one is used. This is on a square plate with a diagonal of 8¹/₄ inches, so you must turn the meeting parts of bowl and base more than this. Thickness of the bearing is about ¹/₄ inch. The method of fitting is with four wood screws into the bottom of the bowl and small bolts or self-tapping screws through the base (Fig. 7-3B). Recess the base to allow for the bolts; this helps the base to stand firmly in its rim. Get the Lazy Susan bearing before turning the wood in case you have to modify sizes.

The large bowl has a flat bottom, which you can screw to a faceplate. Turn it to 14

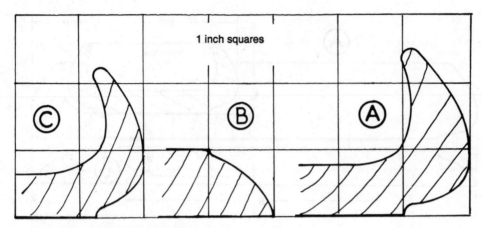

Fig. 7-4. Edge sections for bowl and base parts.

inches in diameter. The rim is 2¹/₂-inches thick. Hollow and shape to the suggested section (Fig. 7-4A) to give an inside diameter of 12 inches. The curve has to clear the small bowls. Keep the bottom flat across, so the small bowls will stand level.

You can turn the base with its upper surface against the faceplate. Turn the outside to shape (Fig. 7-4B). The top diameter should match the bowl bottom. Turn a recess in the lower side to clear the holes needed for the Lazy Susan bearing.

Check the circle sizes for the three bowls to fit inside (Fig. 7-3C). Turn three matching bowls to a section to fit inside the large bowl (Fig. 7-4C).

Mark the hole positions for the bearing, being careful to arrange it central. Drill through the base for the bolts or self-tapping screws; then, use wood screws into the bowl before driving the bolts up through the base. Check the action, then withdraw the bolts so you can get at all parts for staining and polishing. Cloth under the base rim will prevent slipping on a polished table top.

8
Egg Timers

There is a fascination about a sand glass egg timer, although logically it is outdated. Construction depends on the size of the glass part, so this should be obtained first. The reversible turned case of the first example has small parts, so this could be a project to use scraps of attractive wood, and it could be made on the smallest lathe. Many variations are possible, but the usual egg timer (or hour glass in a larger size) has disc ends and three turned pillars (Fig. 8-1). The two end pieces grip the glass, and the pillars are spaced to give a small clearance to the glass part (Fig. 8-2A).

Draw a circle on a piece of paper or card of the greatest size of the glass. Outside this, draw a pitch circle for the pillar positions. Step the radius around this and mark alternate places as holes for the ends of the pillars. Draw another circle outside this as the actual size of an end disc (Fig. 8-2B). Use this drawing as a guide to size when turning the wooden parts.

There can be a shaped hollow in each disc for the glass (Fig. 8-2C) or a shallow hole will do (Fig. 8-2D). Because the timer has to stand on either end, these should be basically flat, although there can be a turned design (Fig. 8-2E).

The pillars look best if their thicker parts are near the center, opposite the narrow part of the glass. The ends can taper to dowels or be shouldered (Fig. 8-2F). If there is a taper without a shoulder, it is possible to have the holes a little too deep and adjust the distance between the discs as you glue so as to firmly hold the glass part. However, be careful that all pillars finish with the same length exposed when glued and the timer stands upright. Shouldering the pillars automatically gets the discs parallel, but does not allow adjustment. A disc of card can be put at an end of the glass if slack has to be taken up.

It is advisable to polish or varnish the wooden parts before assembling with the glass; otherwise, it is difficult to get a satisfactory finish without marking the glass.

TUBULAR EGG TIMER

This type of egg timer has the glass enclosed, and the whole thing must be turned over

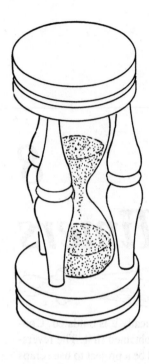

Fig. 8-1. An egg timer made with three pillars doweled into end pieces is shown.

to make the sand run the other way. Sizes will depend on the available glass, but the one shown suits a parallel glass about 3 inches long and $^5/_8$ inch in diameter (Fig. 8-3A). Get your glass first and settle the wood sizes around it (Fig. 8-3B). Any wood can be used, but more care will be needed turning softwoods than the preferable hardwoods.

There are two possible ways of making the egg timer.A tube to fit around the glass could form one part, then separate ends glued on after the glass has been inserted. It is probably better to make the tube and one end as a single piece of wood; then, turn the other end separately. This method is described below.

With this type of assembly, it is always wiser to drill the hole first. Make it an easy fit on the glass, but not so loose that it moves about. There should not be any need to glue or pack the glass. Drilling could be done in the lathe or on a drill press. Freehand drilling with an electric drill is not advised, because the hole produced may not finish truly in line with the wood. Have the piece of wood long enough to allow some waste at the headstock end (Fig. 8-3C).

Turn a plug to support the wood at the tailstock end (Fig. 8-3D). With this arrangement, you can turn the main part to size. Before you part off, check the fit of the glass inside and turn the other end so when the loose part is fitted, it will just touch the end of the glass and hold it.

To avoid having a hole showing in the separate piece, drill a shallow hole for the recess first. Do this so it can be pushed onto a plug of scrap wood mounted on a screw center or in a chuck.

The pair of cutaways in the tubular part should be made with a fine-toothed fretsaw or coping saw. Doing this will keep cleaning up with a file or an abrasive to a minimum. The amount removed should be enough for the state of the sand to be seen, but there is no need

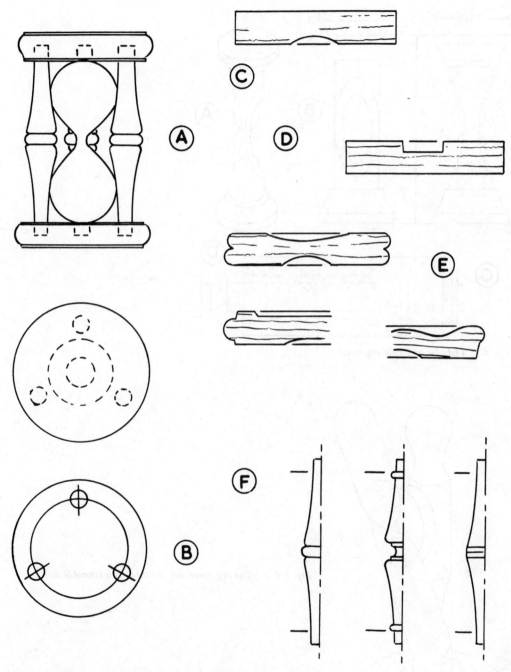

Fig. 8-2. Details for the invertible egg timer shown in Fig. 8-1 are given.

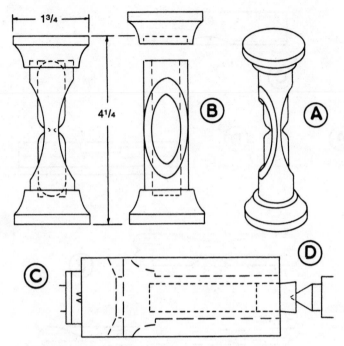

Fig. 8-3. A tubular invertible egg timer.

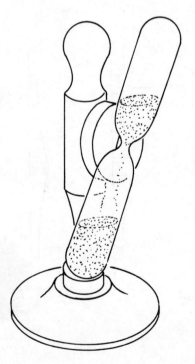

Fig. 8-4. A pillar egg timer with the tube on a rotatable disc.

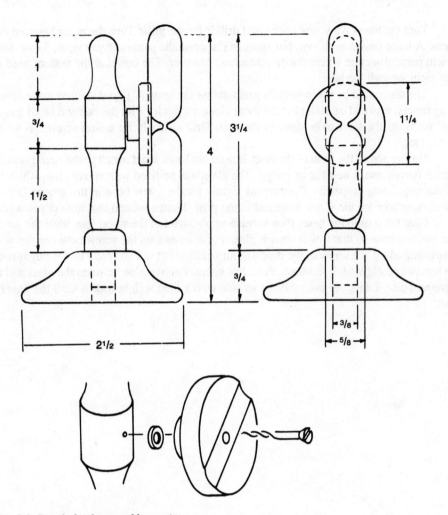

Fig. 8-5. Details for the rotatable egg timer.

to cut far towards the ends of the glass tube. If you want to stain or polish the wood, that is best done before you finally fit the glass and glue on the end. To prevent the timer from slipping on a smooth surface, glue a disc of cloth on each end.

ROTATING EGG TIMER

This egg timer uses a sand glass of the cylindrical type, which is sometimes mounted by its gripped center on a backboard or fitted between two end pieces joined by pillars. In this timer, the glass is mounted on a disc that can be rotated on a pillar projecting from a steady base (Fig. 8-4). The design suits a waisted sand glass about 3¹/₂ inches in diameter, with a timing of 3 to 4 minutes (Fig. 8-5). The disc should be made of close-grained hardwood in order to reduce the risk of the thin section breaking. The other parts can be anything you wish.

Turn the base on a screw center and drill it for the pillar. Turn the pillar between centers. A basic design is shown, but you can elaborate the pattern if you wish. Leave sufficient parallel section where the disc attaches, however. The dowel at the bottom need not go right through the base.

The disc could be made with its grain across or through. If you want to make several egg timers, it would be easier to turn them along a cylinder with the one end faced and cut off ready for the same to be done to the next. Drill centrally for a slim screw 5/8- or 3/4-inch long.

Groove across the front of the disc. It need not be an exact match to the sand glass, but get it fairly close. Use a file or gouge. The glass will be fixed with epoxy glue, which has some gap-filling properties.Countersink lightly for the screw head in the groove.Drill an undersize hole for the screw to thread in the post. Flatten around that hole if you wish.

Glue the post to the base, then varnish or polish all of the wood, but leave the groove in the disc bare so that it will absorb glue. Put a washer on the screw between the wood parts and adjust the screw so the disc will turn easily, but not so freely that it might rotate when you do not wish it to rotate. Put a few spots of epoxy glue between the glass and the grooved disc. Leave the assembly on its side with a light weight over it until the glue has set.

9
Preserves Stand

This is a stand that holds three jars of preserves, jelly, or other foods, together with three spoons, all with a central spindle and a knob handle at the top (Figs. 9-1 and 9-2). The stand could be made to hold four jars, but three will probably take care of most needs. Sizes depend on the jars or pots that are to be held. The height of the spindle will depend on the sizes of spoons to be used. It is best to obtain the spoons and jars first and then design the stand to suit them. As shown, the stand is about 12-inches high and 8-inches across and is made to suit jars about $2^3/4$ inches in diameter and $4^1/2$-inches high with spoons about 7-inches long.

Any close-grained hardwood can be used. There is no fine turning that might produce weak sections in open-grained wood, except for the disc to hold the spoons. If you want to use a weaker wood to match furniture or a table top, that disc might be made of a different close-grained wood in a contrasting color.

The base is shown with a shaped outline. It could be round, but that makes a rather large disc if intended for three jars. If there are to be four, the round area has less blind spaces between the jars, so it does not look so bulky. The base could be made from one piece of wood and the hollows cut with an expanding bit or a hole saw, but it may be easier to make it out of two $1/2$ inch-thicknesses; then, the holes can be cut without any disfiguring marks in their bottoms. However, the bottoms of the holes could be covered with cloth or plastic discs. It would be possible to turn the hollows, but that would mean mounting the wood three times on the faceplate; it would be rotating eccentrically with a risk of vibration and possible damage.

If the base is made in two parts, arrange the two sections 180 degrees to each other and cut the holes in the top part before bandsawing or jigsawing the outline. When this shape is satisfactory, use it to mark on the lower piece. Glue the parts together and shape their combined outlines. Rounding the lower edge lightens appearance. With a suitable cutter a router could be used to mold the edge of the base.

Drill $1/2$-inch holes for the feet and the central spindle. The feet can be turned to any shape you wish, but as they do not show much, a simple outline is sufficient.

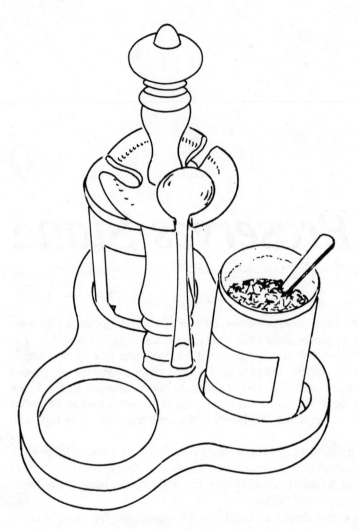

Fig. 9-1. Preserves stand.

The disc for holding the spoons could be turned on a screw center and drilled for the central dowel afterwards. Another way would be to saw the wood circular and drill the dowel hole, so it can be slid onto a slightly tapered mandrel to be mounted between centers. An advantage of this latter method is that the outline must finish concentrically with the hole, where a slight error in drilling in the first method could cause the disc to assemble askew on the other parts. The underside of the disc should be flat where it fits against the main spindle ($1^1/_4$ inches in diameter). The upper surface should be turned hollow with a curve that will blend into the handle part that fits against it (1 inch in diameter). The hollow helps to keep the spoons from falling out of their slots.

Mark the centerlines of the spoon slots at 120 degrees to each other. What size you make the slots depends on the necks of the spoons. As shown, the slots are $^5/_{16}$-inch wide and cut into the bottoms of the hollow. Drill the bottoms of the slots and saw into them. Carefully clean the slot edges and round the entry corners.

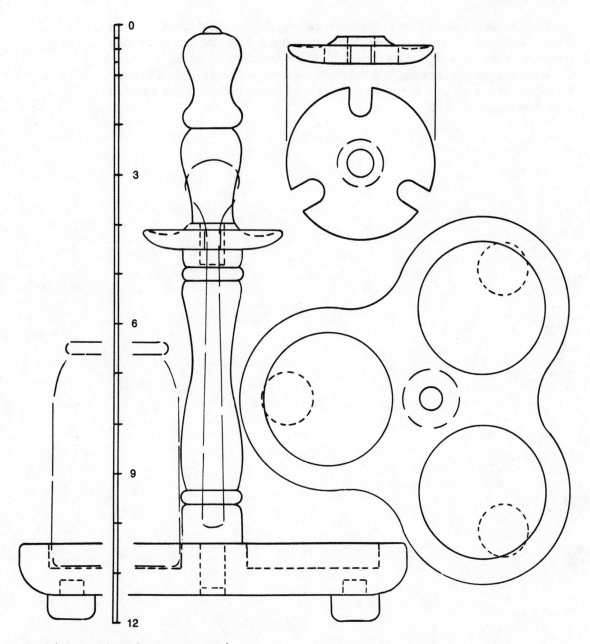

Fig. 9-2. Suggested sizes for a preserves stand.

The main spindle is basically 1 1/4 inches in diameter. It is shown with a narrow neck and two beads, but this is a part where you can use your own ideas, although most of the spindle will be hidden by the spoons and jars. Turn a dowel at the bottom to almost go through the hole in the base, and drill a hole at the top for the peg from the upper part.

The top is shown with a knob 1¹/₄ inches in diameter, but you could turn a larger one if you wish. Make a dowel to go through the spoon disc and into the hole in the main spindle. Turn the lower edge with a curve to blend into the hollow of the disc.

When you glue the parts together, make sure the spoon slots come midway between the hollows to take the jars. A waterproof finish is advisable, because spilled preserves might have to be washed off.

10

Floor Lamp Standard

A stand to support a lamp that could be 60 inches from the floor would be too long to turn in one piece in most lathes. In any case, it is better made in parts. This brings the pieces of wood down to a length that will fit between lathe centers. It also means greater economy, as you do not have to turn away large amounts of waste, if the same piece included thick and thin parts. It also allows easier drilling of a hole the entire length to take wires. Most drills intended for long drilling from the tailstock can cope with depths of about 12 inches, so by drilling from opposite ends you can deal with 24-inch sections. Keeping these hole lengths reasonably short is desirable as a drill may wander out of true if taken too deep.

Joints between parts are not difficult to arrange as a turned dowel or tenon on one piece can fit a hole in the next piece. With both parts of the joint cut on the lathe the sections should automatically finish in line. Beads at the joints disguise the meeting lines.

A tall lamp standard needs a broad and heavy base to resist knocking over. This project (Fig. 10-1) has a base turned, so plenty of wood is left to provide weight; then, the piece next above it is also heavy. Stability is increased further with three extending legs. The rest of the column is in two parts, so there is nothing longer than 23 inches to turn.

A 3/8-inch hole the entire length should be ample to pass wires. Dowels and their holes may be 1 inch in diameter and 1 1/4- inch deep (Fig. 10-2A). The dowels are upward, except at the bottom (Fig. 10-2B). The extreme top is shown cylindrical (Fig. 10-2C), but you will have to make this to suit your chosen lamp and shade fitting.

Materials List for Floor Lamp Standard

1 base	24 × 24 × 3 1/2
3 feet	8 × 3 × 1 1/2
1 section	16 × 6 diameter
2 sections	24 × 4 diameter

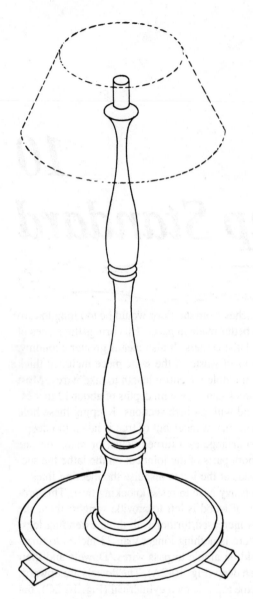

Fig. 10-1. A floor lamp standard with built-up parts.

Settle on a standard width for beads—³/₈ inch would be suitable. Beads of adjoining parts should have matching diameters. The bulbous shapes of the three upright sections should complement each other, with the lower thicker parts proportionately bulkier, which gives a more balanced aesthetic appearance than if the proportion were the other way round.

The base is shown 24 inches in diameter (Fig. 10-2D) and 3¹/₂-inches deep at the center. Its shaping gives a lighter appearance (Fig. 10-3A), but there is actually plenty of bulk to provide weight. Drill the dowel and wire holes through the center. Mark the positions of the three feet underneath.

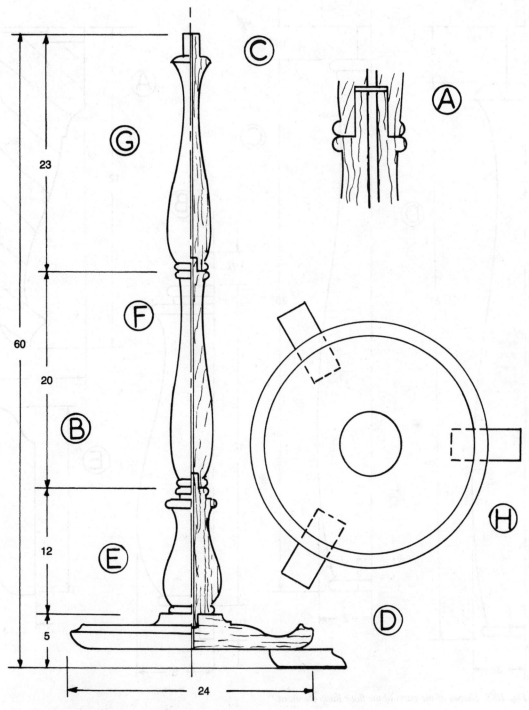

Fig. 10-2. Sizes and sections of the floor lamp standard.

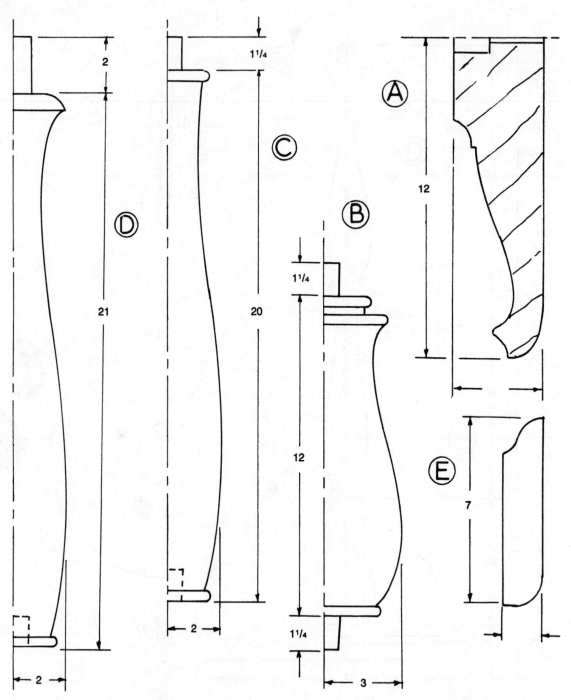

Fig. 10-3. Shapes of the parts of the floor lamp standard.

The bottom section of the pillar (Fig. 10-2E) has dowels at both ends (Fig. 10-3B), but it will be advisable to do most of the other turning before reducing them to size, in case the ends become to weak. The top beads on this piece have a gap between. Make the top bead $3^{1}/_{4}$ inches in diameter to match another on the next section. The other bead may be $4^{1}/_{2}$ inches in diameter. Drill the wire hole and make the dowels to fit a test hole in a piece of scrap wood.

The middle section (Fig. 10-2F) has a hole at the bottom and its own dowel at the top (Fig. 10-3C). The beads at both ends may be $3^{1}/_{2}$ inches in diameter. Drill the wire hole from both ends.

Turn the top section (Fig. 10-2G) with a hole and bead to match the section below. Prepare the top to suit your lamp fitting. There is a flare below that (Fig. 10-3D) and shaping it may be a little slimmer than the pattern below, for the sake of appearance. Drill the wire hole from both ends.

The feet (Figs. 10-2H and 10-3E) are flat and 3-inches wide. Shape the outer end and round the inner end. Glue and screw below the base.

As you assemble the parts, it will be advisable to thread the electric wires into each section, or put in a plain wire that can be used to pull the others through. Otherwise, you may have difficulty in pushing wire through the whole length and there may be a risk of the hole becoming blocked **with** glue at the joints.

Join the top two sections first and check their straightness on the bench. Add the third section and again check straightness. Join this assembly to the base, while that is on a level surface. View from several directions to see that the lamp standard is upright.

Stain and varnish or polish the lamp standard after completion; consider dealing with each part in the lathe. It is possible to get a good finish with a friction polish, such as wax of shellac, while the wood is rotating.

11
Round Table

In earlier days a small round table was called a candle stand because its main use was supporting a candle at a suitable height for reading. Such a table may now be used beside a chair for books, knitting or a table lamp. It may also serve as a stand for a plant in a pot or flowers in a vase.

The round top on a central pillar was sometimes supported on three sawn feet or on a tripod arrangement of three turned legs, as in the example (Fig. 11-1). All parts for this design are made on a lathe. Any hardwood might be used. It would be possible to use a softwood, but then it would be difficult to turn sharp outlines and there would be a risk of the top warping or cracking.

The suggested sizes (Fig. 11-2A) could be modified if you want a different height. Lengths of the pillar and legs are easy to alter. When viewed from above, make sure the legs extend at least as far as the circumference of the top (Fig. 11-2B).

The top has a flat underside, so the planed wood disc may be turned in one operation on a faceplate. Reduce the $1^{1}/_{4}$-inch thickness to $^{3}/_{4}$ inch over the central area, to leave enough wood for stiffness, with a $^{1}/_{2}$-inch-high rim (Fig. 11-3A). Draw a circle on the bottom to mark the position of the pad.

The pad under the top is turned to bed against it and with a 1-inch hole for the pillar

---

Materials List for Round Table

1 top	14×14	$\times 1^{1}/_{4}$
1 pad	6×6	$\times 1^{1}/_{4}$
1 base block	6×6	$\times 3$
1 pillar	$18 \times$	$2^{1}/_{2}$ diameter
3 legs	$12 \times$	2 diameter

Fig. 11-1. A round table with all turned parts.

dowel (Fig. 11-3B). All of the dowels turned in this table may be 1 inch in diameter and 1-inch long.

The pillar has a maximum $2^1/2$ inches in diameter and retains this full diameter as cylinders at the end. The bulbous part should also be near this full diameter (Fig. 11-3C). Turn the 1-inch dowels on the ends.

The base block (Fig. 11-2D) forms the joint between the pillar and the legs. Assembling the stand upright and symmetrical depends on the accuracy of these joints, so careful drilling is important (Fig. 11-2E). Turn the block (Figs. 11-2F and 11-3D) to the outline shown. The slope of the bottom is 30 degrees so the legs will be at 60 degrees to the ground. While the block is in the lathe, pencil or cut a circle on the bottom slope for locating the leg holes. Step off the radius around this circle to accurately obtain the centers of the three holes (Fig. 11-3E). Drill the holes square to the block slope. Drill a central hole on top for the dowel of the pillar.

Made three identical legs (Fig. 11-3F) with dowels to fit the base block and elliptical ends to form feet.

If the pad is glued under the top with its grain across that of the top, this will reduce the risk of warping. Glue those two parts and the legs into the base block before joining the assembly with the pillar. If the top does not finish level and the pillar upright, you may take a little off one leg, but with careful cutting and drilling that should not be necessary.

Apply a finish appropriate to the wood or to match surrounding furniture.

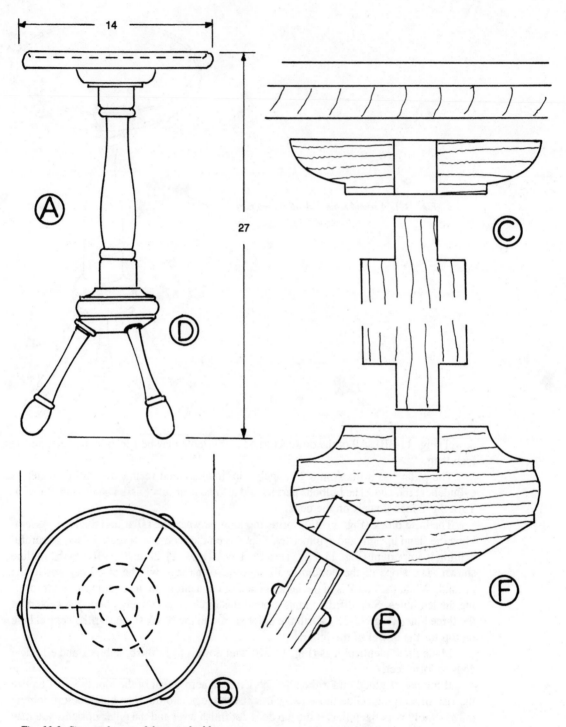

Fig. 11-2. Sizes and parts of the round table.

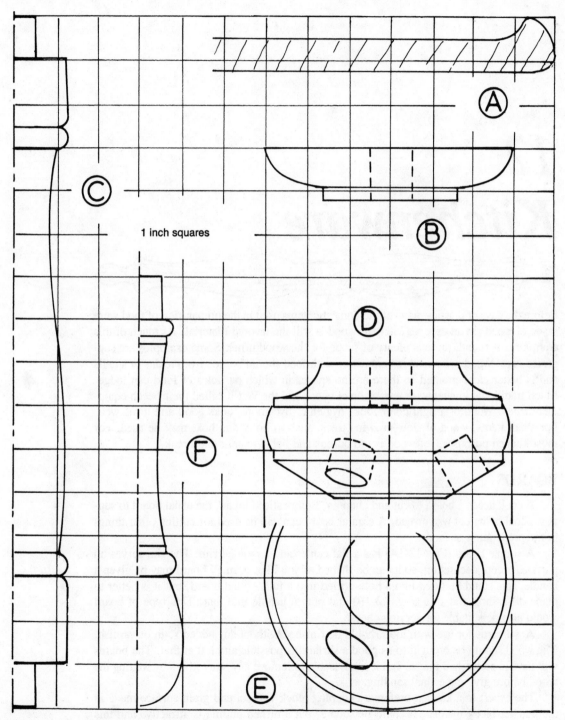

Fig. 11-3. Suggested shapes for parts of the round table.

12
Kitchenware

Before the days of plastics many of the domestic items used in the preparation of food were made of wood. In an expert's kitchen, wood is still the favored material. As much of this equipment is round, there is plenty of scope for the woodturner. Some examples are suggested here. Wood to be used in connection with food should be free from resins or smells and is better close-grained so there are no spaces in which particles of food can lodge. Much traditional kitchenware was made of beech and the Welsh called their beech equipment *treen*. Wood of a light color looks hygienic. Sycamore looks good and turns well. For small items, wood of slow-growing trees, such as holly and box, may be used. For most kitchen purposes, softwood is too porous and liable to split and break.

BOARDS

A cook needs a board to cut and chop on. Before sliced bread, the usual board to support a loaf being cut was turned. A similar board can still be used for cutting other things in the preparation of food.

A simple board (Fig. 12-1A) has a flat center and a molded rim. The rim serves no purpose except decoration, so it can be shaped as you like. A small board may be given a handle. This could be fitted into a hole drilled into a fully-round board, but it is better to plane off a short flat side (Fig. 12-1B) and plug a handle into that. This type of board would also be suitable for serving cheese.

Any boards for use with food should be finished without any added stain or varnish. The wood should be brought to as good a surface as possible and left at that. The boards will have to be washed in use, and it is advisable to remove any stray fibers by wetting the wood before giving the final sanding.

The expert in a kitchen prefers a chopping block with an end grain surface made in the butcher block manner. It could be square, but a turned outline is attractive and this allows a small amount of rounding of the edges, which makes handling easier. Obviously the wood must be a type that is safe with food, and it should be hard and close-grained to

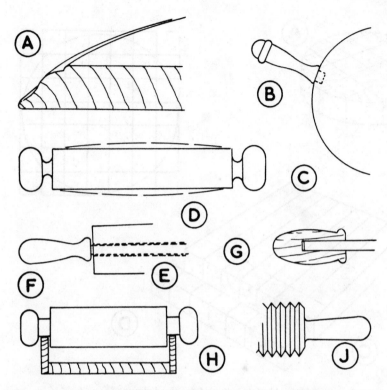

Fig. 12-1. Bread boards and variations on the rolling pin can be made on the lathe.

resist heavy chopping blows. Sizes can range from about 6-inches up to quite large boards for professional use. The specimen suggested (Fig. 12-2A) could be made of 1¹/₂ inch-square pieces to give a board about 10 inches in diameter with seven squares across.

A pattern of squares with a circle drawn on them (Fig. 12-2B) shows that the corner blocks are not needed. Although, you may prefer to include them in the first assembly, particularly if you are using wood of other sections. This is an opportunity to use odd pieces of wood, not necessarily square, although they should all be the same width. For instance, you could adopt 1¹/₂ inches as a standard width but might then include strips thinner or thicker to make up the size the other way.

If the block is to have seven squares across the diameter each way, prepare enough strips to cut the seven pieces. Whatever size squares you use, allow for the finished board to be at least 1¹/₂-inches thick (Fig. 12-2C). You will notice (Fig. 12-2B) that with the size of the board and the squares suggested, you could use only five strips and allow for cutting off seven parts. Join the strips together. Use a waterproof glue. When the glue has set, level the surfaces, and then cut off enough sets of blocks (Fig. 12-2D). Glue these edge-to-edge to make up a big enough area to let you draw the circle. Saw a disc ready for mounting on the lathe.

The cook will want to use both sides of the block. You could mount it with screws through a packing on the faceplate, and then plug the screw holes later. Or, another way would be to plane one end-grain surface flat, and then mount it by gluing it to a wood block on the faceplate with paper in the joint, so that it can be eased off after turning. That

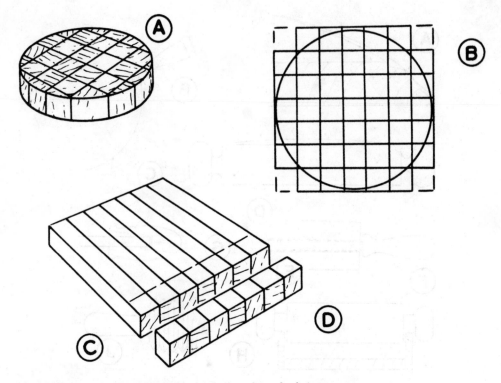

Fig. 12-2. An end-grain chopping block is built up from glued pieces.

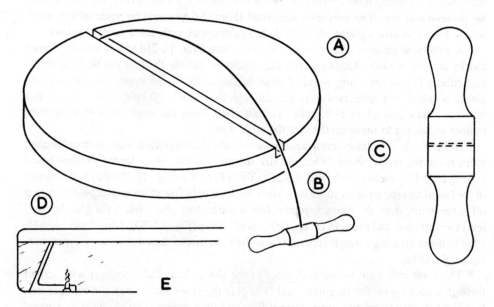

Fig. 12-3. A cheese cutting board uses a wire through a groove.

allows you to turn the rim and the other surface. Besides sanding on the lathe, the two working surfaces should be rubbed smooth on a piece of abrasive paper resting on a flat surface.

Before it is used, it is advisable to sufficiently soak the wood in vegetable cooking oil to impregnate the grain. This will reduce any tendency to split or warp and will be hygienic for working with food.

CHEESE CUTTING BOARD

The expert way to cut cheese is with a wire on a grooved cutting board. The board may be any size, but the suggested size is about 9 inches in diameter and 1 inch thick (Fig. 12-3A). The wood should be close-grained and safe for use with food. The cheese board could be built up from square pieces, as described for the chopping block, if you want to make matching kitchen equipment; otherwise, this is unnecessary and a board with its grain across is suitable. If you can find a quarter-sawn piece of wood (with the end grain lines about square to the broad surface), there will be less risk of warping, but any properly-seasoned piece of wood should keep its shape without giving trouble in use.

Saw the disc and turn it on a pad on the faceplate. The underside will not normally be seen, so you can screw on and plug the holes later. Round the circumference edges slightly. How the groove is cut depends on your equipment. Size is not critical, but 1/4 inch wide and 1/4 inch deep would be suitable. With a router you may be able to cut a groove with a rounded bottom.

The cutting wire should be spring steel and not thicker than 20 gauge. Ideally, this should be stainless steel, but more likely it will be plain steel, often sold as "piano" wire. Model shops may have it. A length of twice the diameter of the board will be more than enough (Fig. 12-3B).

You can make the handle how you wish, but a simple form is shown (Fig. 12-3C). It is 3/4 inch in diameter and 4 inches long to give a comfortable grip. Take the wire through a central hole, and bend the wire over its end to drive it into the wood.

At the end of the groove across the board, drill a hole no bigger than necessary to clear the wire. Do this at a moderate angle in the direction of the pull (Fig. 12-3D); then, groove along a short way underneath to where the wire can be trapped under a screw head (Fig. 12-3E).

The board may be left untreated, so it can be washed occasionally, or it could be wiped over with vegetable oil to provide a finish. Let the oil dry completely before cutting cheese, so the taste is not affected. To use the board, put a piece of cheese centrally on it with the wire out of the way; then lower the wire into the end of the groove and pull down. You can get a cleaner cut on most cheeses than you can get with a knife.

ROLLING PIN

Expert cooks prefer a wooden roller for working on pastry, and many prefer the roller be made in one piece with knobs at the ends (Figs. 12-1C and 12-4). The roller may be parallel for most of its length with a slight curving at the ends, or it may be made slightly bulbous (Fig. 12-1D). Both types have their uses in food preparation.

With the one-piece roller, the end knobs have to be allowed to turn in the hand. An

Fig. 12-4. A rolling pin is a simple spindle turning project.

alternative is to let the roller revolve on an axle with handles at the ends (Fig. 12-1E). The roller is turned and drilled through with a hole that will make a loose fit on the axle. If it is necessary to drill from both ends, leave some waste wood on each end to accommodate the driving center until after the hole has been made. The axle may be turned with one of the handles, with an extension to fit in the other handle (Fig. 12-1F). An alternative is to use prepared dowel rod for the axle, and drill both handles to take it (Fig. 12-1G).

Basically similar rollers were used for other domestic purposes. One with parts to run along guides at the edge of a wooden tray was used in butter making (Fig. 12-1H). An oatmeal roller is made in either of the ways just described, but its surface is ribbed (Fig. 12-1J).

PESTLE AND MORTAR

A pestle and mortar was once an essential part of kitchen equipment. It still is needed by anyone preparing food from natural materials straight from the field. It serves two functions: pounding grain and similar things to powder and mixing assorted powders. Even if rarely used today, the pair make an interesting kitchen decoration as well as a challenging project for a woodturner.

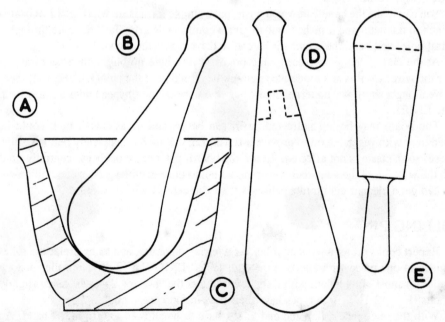

Fig. 12-5. A pestle and mortar.

The mortar is a stout wooden bowl (Fig. 12-5A). The inside is the important part. This should have a curve slightly more than that of a bottom of the pestle.

The pestle needs to be fairly heavy (Fig. 12-5B). It is given a taper and a knob handle. The bottom should have a curve slightly less than that of a bottom of the mortar (Fig. 12-5C). The middle of the end of the pestle should always make contact with the inside of the mortar at any angle it is held. It would not do its job properly if the curve of its bottom was flattened.

An interesting alternative way of making the pestle is to use two woods. The lower part is heavier, while the top part can be a lighter wood of attractive appearance. The two pieces are first turned cylindrical with a substantial dowel on one piece mating with a hole

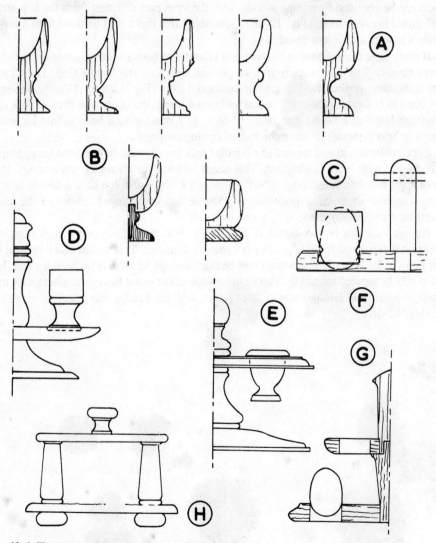

Fig. 12-6. The variety of egg cups and egg stands are infinite.

in the other (Fig. 12-5D), then the shape is turned after they have been glued together. The joint should come above the rim of the mortar when the pestle is placed in it.

A pestle is not very different from a mallet. It is possible to make this a dual tool by rounding the end of a mallet so it can act as a pestle (Fig. 12-5E). The mortar should be wide enough to provide some clearance around the mallet, which needs to be moved to angles a little each side of vertical.

EGGCUPS AND RACKS

Eggcups are popular turning projects. A selection of designs are shown here (Fig. 12-6A). The choice is broadly between those with stems and those that are lower. Interesting effects can be obtained by mixing woods, with the stem part different from the cup and a small dowel between them (Fig. 12-6B). Something like this could be done with a lower cup on a base of a different wood.

If many eggs in cups have to be moved, it is useful to have a stand to accommodate the normal number. This may range from a simple disc with a central handle (Fig. 12-6C) to a more elaborately turned stand following traditional lines (Fig. 12-6D). Usually, the eggcups stand in hollows in the disc. In one traditional stand, the cups have rims so they can fit through holes in a raised disc (Fig. 12-6E). Any stand with a base should be broad enough or heavy enough to make the risk of tipping minimal.

Eggs can be stored and carried in a circular rack very similar to one used for eggcups. A single disc with holes is simplest. This needs feet to give clearance underneath. One ring of holes may be enough (Fig. 12-6F), although a larger disc can have a double ring of holes, staggered so as many positions as possible can be arranged. Holes of the sizes needed are most cleanly made with a saw tooth bit.

An egg rack can be two-tiered (Fig. 12-6G). Placing and removing eggs from the lower part is facilitated if the upper tier is a smaller diameter. This means that there can be more holes in the bottom. The bottom may be thick enough so there is no need for feet, but the top may be tapered toward the rim so the overall effect is not heavy. An alternative to a central pedestal is an arrangement of three pillars with the handle only attached to the top disc (Fig. 12-6H).

13
Dresser or Desk Set

There is usually a need for a great many containers of various sorts on a dresser or anywhere used as a dressing table, and all of these can be made by a woodturner. Many similar items, although for different uses, can be used on a desk. Some of them may also be used by an artist, anyone enjoying a hobby involving many small things, or by a cook in the kitchen. The items described here are particularly related to a dresser, but the alternative uses will be apparent.

Although you might attempt to use uniform design characteristics for the sake of a balanced appearance to the set, this is not quite so important as may be thought, as the fact that everything is round may give enough similarity to make the whole collection look a set. It also helps to use the same wood throughout or stain different woods to match. For articles made of more than one part use contrasting woods. For instance, a ring stand could have a light-colored stem, while the lower part retained a balanced visual appearance by being made of the same wood as other items.

A good close-grained hardwood with interesting grain markings would be a good choice. As none of the items are large, you may be able to find pieces of rarer woods, which are unavailable in larger sizes.

A selection of articles are shown (Fig. 13-1). You do not have to make everything at one time, but you can build up the set at intervals. However, if you are using an uncommon wood, make sure you have enough for all parts.

The most general need is for one or more small bowls (Fig. 13-2A). It may be advisable to make a pair at the same time. Whatever the outside shape, make the inside to a smooth curve flared outwards (Fig. 13-2B), so you can use your fingers to scoop anything out over the side. You should be able to turn a bowl on a screw center or a small faceplate. Cloth on the finished bowl will hide the hole.

A ring stand can be made to match the basic bowl. Turn it in the same way, but leave a projection at the center (Fig. 13-2C). The size of the projection depends on the stem. Rings do not have to fit tightly, so a taper from about $1/2$ inch to $1/4$ inch should be satisfac-

Fig. 13-1. Turned items for use on a dresser or desk.

tory. Turn the stem with a dowel to fit a hole in the bowl projection. Blend the curves of the two parts into each other (Fig. 13-2D), or turn a bead where they join (Fig. 13-2E), which will hide any slight differences in size.

The bowl below gives the ring stand a second use, but if you only need a stand for rings, fit the stem to a base (Fig. 13-3A). Turn the whole thing in one piece, but that means cutting away a lot of wood to waste. It might be better to turn the base on a screw center and the stem between centers. You could produce a pair of his and her ring stands.

Further developments of this design are stands for bracelets and necklaces. For hanging bracelets, the stem must be taken up to an enlarged top, into which two or three pegs are doweled (Fig. 13-3B). All of this has to be fairly slender, so it looks graceful, but the loads are slight. Holes for the pegs will run into each other and need care in drilling, but when the parts are glued there will be ample mutual strength. The stem could be continued so rings may be held as well as bracelets.

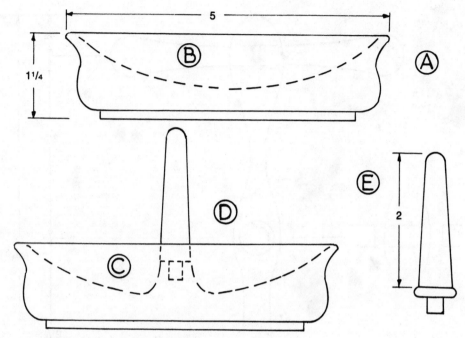

Fig. 13-2. Sizes for a small bowl and a ring stand.

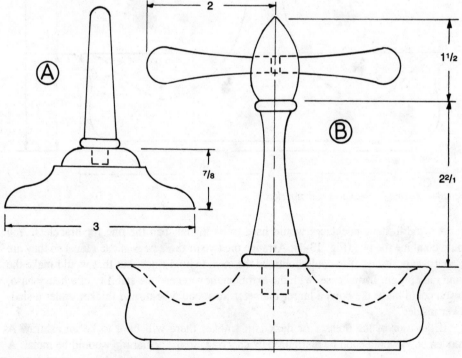

Fig. 13-3. A ring stand and a bracelet stand.

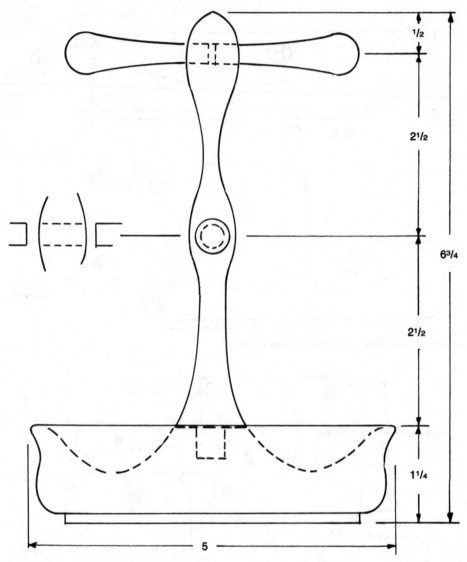

Fig. 13-4. A stand for necklaces and bracelets.

A stand to hang necklaces would have to be higher than the one for bracelets. You could combine the two (Fig. 13-4). Arrange the two or three pegs at each level so they are in alternate positions. You could continue the stem to hold rings, but that would make the stand rather high. In any case, with the extra height you need the stability of a heavy base, so you could make the bowl a larger diameter, or it could be turned thicker under a shallower inside.

If the user of the dresser or desk is a smoker there will have to be an ashtray. A wooden bowl would soon be disfigured by charring, so the actual tray should be metal. A

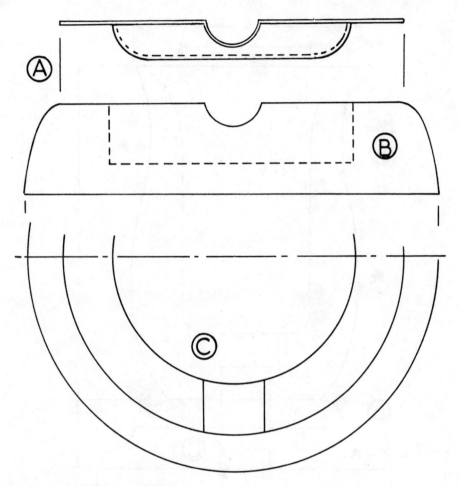

Fig. 13-5. A wood base for a metal ashtray.

simple pressed sheet metal ashtray would be suitable for mounting on a wood base to match other articles. The size of wood will depend on the metal tray you use, but one about 5-inches across should do. It will usually have two or three grooves pressed in the flat rim (Fig. 13-5A).

The base may be a turned block with a hollow to match the tray, but there is no need for an exact fit and the block is shown turned deeper (Fig. 13-5B). Turn the block so its outer edge curves close to the metal tray size. Use a gouge or round file to make the hollows in the wood to take the shaped tray (Fig. 13-5C). Glue the tray to the block with epoxy adhesive.

You will want one or more upright containers to hold long things, such as brushes and files on a dresser or pens on a desk. A pair of these containers will be decorative, whether you have enough things to fill them or not.

In this design (Fig. 13-6) the main container has its grain upright (Fig. 13-6A), the base may be turned with its grain across (Fig. 13-6B) and these parts are joined with a

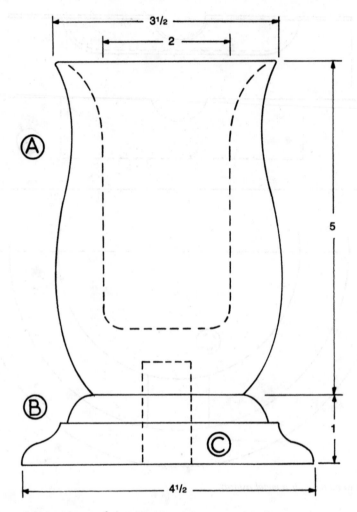

Fig. 13-6. An upright container made in two parts.

separate dowel (Fig. 13-6C). The outline of the main part matches the bowls and the base matches the ring holder.

The inside may be turned to any section, but the parallel form with a flared top gives plenty of capacity.

All of these parts should be given a finish that will withstand handling and should match in appearance. You may need to stain before polishing.

In most cases the set will be used on a polished surface. You could plug any holes and sand level, then leave the surface unpolished, but it would be better to glue on discs of felt or other cloth to reduce slipping and prevent marking the dresser or desk top.

Materials List for Dresser or Desk Set

Tray
1 piece   5 × 5   × 1¹/₄

Tray/Ring Stand
1 piece   5 × 5   × 1¹/₄
1 piece   4 ×   ³/₄ diameter

Ring Stand
1 piece   3 × 3   × ⁷/₈
1 piece   4 ×   ³/₄ diameter

Bracelet Stand
1 piece   5 × 5   × 1¹/₄
1 piece   6 ×   ³/₄ diameter
2 pieces   3 ×   ¹/₂ diameter

Necklace Stand
1 piece   5 × 5   × 1¹/₄
1 piece   7 ×   ³/₄ diameter
2 pieces   3 ×   ¹/₂ diameter

Ashtray
1 piece   6 × 6   × 1

Upright Container
1 piece   4¹/₂ × 4¹/₂ × 1
1 piece   6   × 3¹/₂ diameter

14
Lamp Pendant

Before the days of electric lighting, illumination was by candles, oil, or gas lamps. In important large rooms there was often a candelabra hanging from the ceiling. Many of these were extremely elaborate and carried a large number of candles. The idea has carried over to today, with hanging pendants holding several electric lamps in place of using a single overhead lamp. The number of lamps is usually three or four. A turned fitting can be made with either arrangement, but this project shows three (Fig. 14-1). It would not be difficult to adapt to four if you prefer that arrangement.

The lamp holders are shown upwards, so the lamps and their shades come above the supporting arms. Reverse the arrangement on the ends of the arms to the lamps and shades are downwards. Consider the height of the room and the head clearance there will be under the pendant. Use decorative lamps, such as imitation candles, and dispense with the shades.

Sizes suggested (Fig. 14-2A) should look right in an average room, but you may wish to experiment with the lamps and shades you intend to use and arrange sizes to suit. Any hardwood could be used.

The whole project can be turned. All sections are round, except the ends of the arms (Fig. 14-2B), which are $1^1/2$-inches square. The parts join together with dowels turned on

Materials List for Lamp Pendant

1 central disc	$4 \times 4 \quad \times 1^3/4$
1 spindle	$12 \times 1^7/8$ diameter
3 arms	$12 \times 1^1/2 \times 1^1/2$
3 lamp bases	$3 \times 1^1/2$ diameter
3 plugs	$1 \times 1 \quad$ diameter
1 terminal	$2 \times 1^1/2$ diameter

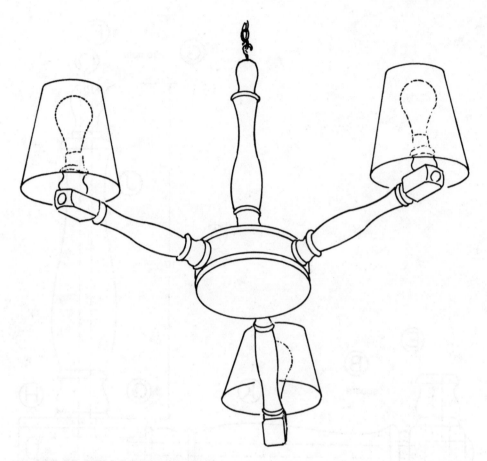

Fig. 14-1. A hanging pendant for three lamps.

them fitting into holes. The wiring holes through the parts may be $^3/_8$ inch, but the holes for dowels are larger and extend to allow you space to manipulate the wires. At the center the dowels and holes may be $^7/_8$ inch, where you need space to deal with three-way wiring (Figs. 14-2C and 14-3A). The central hole goes through the disc and is closed by a terminal after wiring has been fitted (Figs. 14-2D and 14-3B).

At the end of each arm the dowel holes may be reduced to $^3/_4$ inch. They run into each other, which should give you enough space for threading through the wiring. A dowelled plug closes the hole (Fig. 14-3C).

A lamp base is shown with just a wire hole through (Fig. 14-2E), but you will have to open that out if you use a screw-in lamp holder.

The pendant hangs by an eye screw (Fig. 14-2F) into a ring in the ceiling or to a chain. The screw goes into a plug in the wire hole and another hole is drilled diagonally to feed the wire in from the side. As you make parts, bear in mind the need to thread wires through. See that holes are clean and there are no ragged edges around the holes.

The key piece, to which the extending parts fit, is the central disc (Figs. 14-2H and 14-3D), which is 1$^3/_4$-inches thick and cylindrical with beaded edges. Lay out the

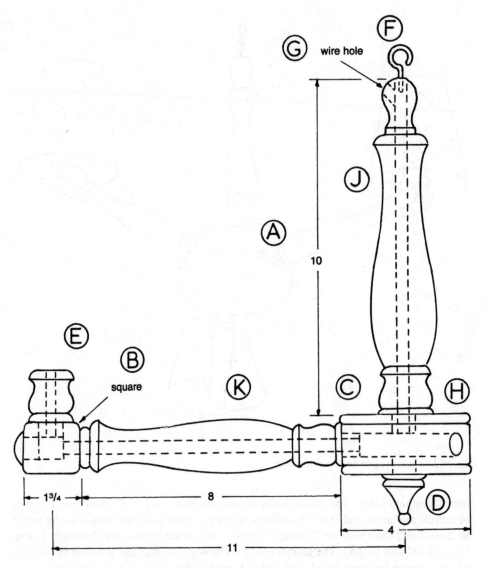

Fig. 14-2. Suggested sizes for the lamp pendant.

equally-spaced hole positions (Fig. 14-3E). Drill the central hole, then the other holes into it.

Make the central spindle (Figs. 14-2J and 14-3F). It has a hole right through and a dowel to fit the central disc hole. Its maximum diameter at the bulbous part is $1^7/8$ inches, but the shaping of the other parts contribute to a more slender appearance. Drill the diagonal wire hole at the top (Fig. 14-2G).

The three arms (Figs. 14-2K and 14-3G) are turned from $1^1/2$-inch-square stock, with that left as the section at the outer end (Fig. 14-2B). The dowel end and the hole through are the same as on the central spindle. Make the maximum turned diameter about $1^3/8$ inches. Drill across and into the square end with $3/4$-inch holes.

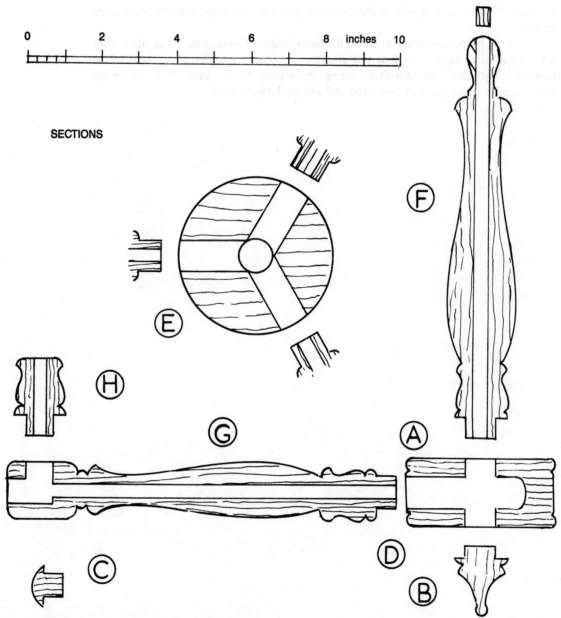

Fig. 14-3. Sections and shapes of parts of the lamp pendant.

A lamp base (Figs. 14-2E and 14-3H) has an outline the same as the inner end of an arm, with a dowel to penetrate as far as the hole from the end.

Turn the terminal to press into the bottom hole after you have passed through the wiring (Figs. 14-2D and 14-3B). Make three plugs to close the end holes (Fig. 14-3C).

You will find it easiest to thread wires through parts loosely as you prepare to assemble them. Fit the central spindle to the disc; then, add the three arms, with the wires taken through.

Have the lamp bases ready to attach the lamp holders. Connect the wires, then work the surplus wires back through as you glue the lamp bases into the square ends of the arms. When you are satisfied with the wiring, fit the plugs and the terminal. Close the top of the spindle with a piece of dowel rod and add the hanging hook.

15
Children's
Games and Toys

Before the days of mass-produced toys, when everyone was more dependent on what could be produced locally, the wheelwright or other woodworker with a lathe, kept children supplied with such things as spinning tops and skipping rope handles. In this modern quantity-producing world there is still an attraction about an individually made toy. There are a great many toys which can be turned, often from pieces of wood too small for anything else. Even if you only have the smallest lathe, you can supply all the neighborhood children with toys. It is surprising how many toys or things for children's games are, or could be, turned. Some suggestions follow, but you should be able to discover many more.

SPINNING TOPS

Spinning tops to be whipped are certainly simple things to turn (Fig. 15-1A). For durability, finish with a round-headed nail.

A further step is to make a top that can be spun by pulling a cord (Fig. 15-1B). The body for the top should be heavy wood for the longest spin and have its weight concentrated in the greatest diameter fairly low. The groove for the cord should be smooth, particularly around the edges, so the cord does not snag as it is pulled.

Make the handle in one piece with the dowel, or a piece of hardwood dowel rod might be let into a hole. It would also be possible to use a metal rod instead of the dowel rod. In any case, the bore of the top hole should be quite a loose fit. If the top is drilled right through, the point can be another piece of dowel or turned rod glued in the bottom with a round-headed nail driven in the end. Sizes may suit available wood, but a diameter of about 5 inches and a height just a little less should give a long spin, which is what the younger user expects.

Another way to make a top spin by pulling a cord is to give the top a stem instead of a hole (Fig. 15-1C). A handle is turned to fit over this, with a slot, to clear the cord wound around the stem (Fig. 15-1D). The stem might be a metal rod going right through the top

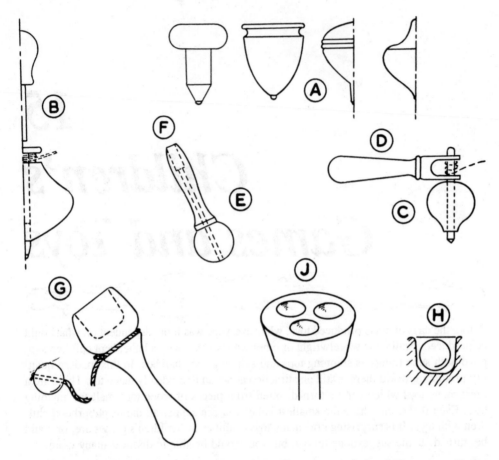

Fig. 15-1. Many children's toys can be turned on a lathe. Those shown include spinning tops, a skipping rope handle, and a ball game.

to a rounded point, or it can be a hardwood dowel. Any pattern can be used for the top, providing it is a large enough diameter to give a flywheel effect.

An example of this type is based on a traditional design (Fig. 15-2). The young owner puts the stem of his top through the hole in the handle, then puts the string through the hole and winds it on several turns. With a good pull, he sets the top spinning and releases it to continue for some time. The drawing shows a top small enough to put in a pocket (Fig. 15-3). It could be bigger, and the design altered, but remember that a top spins like a flywheel, and it needs weight towards its circumference to keep it going, so there must be a bulbous part. Use close-grained hardwood to stand up to rough use.

Turn the top with the bulbous part stopping at a shoulder where the parallel stem starts. The bottom tapers to a point. For use indoors, a wood curved point will probably be sufficiently durable. If the top is to be used outdoors on stone, there should be a metal end. Make the metal end by driving a nail into a slightly undersize hold, which might be good enough without further treatment, but it is better to turn the head after driving it into

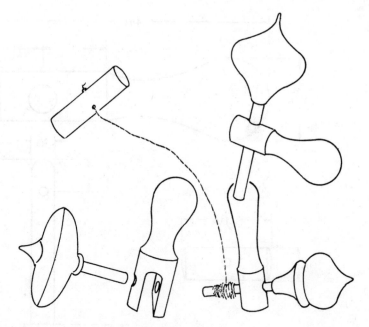

Fig. 15-2. A group of spinning tops based on a traditional design.

the wood. A nail with a thick head gives you more to work on. Shaping could be with a file or a graver, followed by abrasive paper.

Drill the hole in the handle to be quite a loose fit on the stem of the top. The string grip may be a piece of dowel rod, or turn it more shapely. It might be made as a ball or bead. It is best to use flexible braided synthetic cord, 18 inches or longer. Drill a hole at the top of the stem so it slides through easily. Lightly countersink each side for a quick release. Do the same through the grip. Put the end of the string through the hole in the stem, and turn it some more and pull hard in order to prove that your top works.

SKIPPING ROPE HANDLE

A skipping rope handle (Fig. 15-1E) is an interesting turning project. A pair is needed, so there will have to be some careful checking to see that the second handle matches the first. In the traditional shape, a total length of about 5 inches and a diameter of about $1^3/4$ inches should suit the young user's hands. The thickest part of the grip should not be too much to circle with the fingers—probably 1 inch in diameter.

The actual rope should be used as a guide to hole sizes, with a bore to slide easily over the rope and an enlarged end to clear a knot in it (Fig. 15-1F). Attractive wood could be varnished, but the usual finish is paint in a bright color.

BALL AND CUP

Rather similar in appearance to the skipping rope handle is a ball and cup (Fig. 15-1G). A few centuries ago this was a popular toy with adults as well as children. The object is to swing the ball on its string and catch it in the cup. The ball determines the size

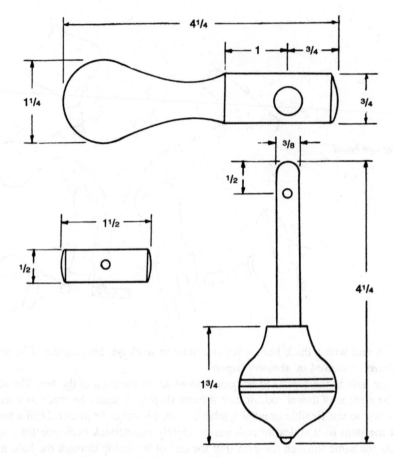

Fig. 15-3. Suggested sizes for a spinning top and handle.

of the other part, but a 1-inch ball is usually standard and the other part made from wood 6×2 inches would be satisfactory.

The ball is drilled to be fairly tight on a piece of cord about 2-feet long. The handle is usually shaped like a skipping rope handle. The size of the cup depends on the degree of skill intended in catching, but there should be a reasonable clearance on the ball. The hollow should certainly be deeper than the diameter of the ball and a clearance of upwards of 1/4 inch is reasonable, possibly more if the user will be a young child (Fig. 15-1H).

A variation is an end with more than one cup (Fig. 15-1J), so more skill is needed to catch the ball in the intended cup.

DIABOLO

Another game that was favored by adults as well as children was "Diavolo" or "Diabolo," which seems to have had a French origin. A cord is fixed between two handles. This is used to control a sort of spool (Fig. 15-4A), which could be tossed and spun by manipulating the handles.

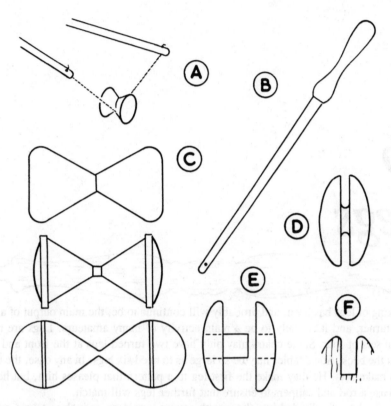

Fig. 15-4. Diabolo is a game that can be made on the lathe as is the yo-yo.

The handles might be straight dowel rods, or have shaped handles and tapered stems, with the cord fixed through holes (Fig. 15-4B). Several variations on the spool are possible, but the essential feature in the design is large heavy ends and a quite small center (Fig. 15-4C). The spool has to revolve along a taut cord or settle with its center on the cord if tossed. Obviously, the center should not be turned too small so the spool breaks if dropped, but aim at the smallest diameter that will still retain strength.

YO-YO

A modern toy with family connections to diabolo is the yo-yo. Various diameters are possible, but 3 inches is reasonable. The whole thing can be turned in one piece like a chalk line reel (Fig. 15-4D), or two discs may be mounted on a piece of dowel rod (Fig. 15-4E). The width between the disc sides should do no more than give a reasonable clearance to the cord, but the faces should be smooth and the outer edge rounded (Fig. 15-4F). It might be easier to get good inner surfaces if the dowel assembly is used.

16
Legs

The making of legs has been, and probably will continue to be, the main output of a commercial turner, and it is likely to be a main activity of many amateurs. Legs are nearly always in sets of four. Some chairs may only have two turned legs at the front and other shapes at the back. Some tables may be so large as to need six legs. In any case, the turner needs to make sets. He may make the first leg to a pattern that pleases him, but he then needs to use a rod and calipers to ensure that further legs will match.

Legs are broadly divided into those with square tops deep enough to take a rail and wide enough to provide stiffness, and those that are expected to take rails lower down. In most cases, there are square sections where the joints come, although a few legs are needed round throughout their length. This occurs with Windsor chairs and others of that type, where a round leg has a dowel top into the seat (Fig. 16-1A). Lower rails also have ends that dowel into the round legs.

Some legs are made of softwoods. These do not take such fine detail as hardwoods. They also tend to be thicker for the sake of strength. Softwood legs may be used in tables that are more useful than beautiful, but some decoration is still welcomed. Many lathes have a capacity about 30 inches between centers.This is to accommodate table legs. A softwood table leg with a top up to 4-inches square is as much as most of the lighter lathes will take. A hardwood leg of this size might be managed, but the work could be tedious due to the need to take light cuts.

For softwood legs, there should be bold outlines and no prominent turning of thin section that might soon suffer from knocks (Fig. 16-1B). Rely on fairly broad beads and flowing curves that do not leave thinner edges outstanding. Although the foot looks more graceful if it tapers to a small size, it has to take all of the weight with its partners and this is better fairly broad (Fig. 16-1C).

The proportion of the lower square, if there is one, needs care. It looks best if its length is at least as much as its width. Too shallow a depth is not usually as attractive. The ends of the square part can be cut square (Fig. 16-1D), but taking off the corners softens

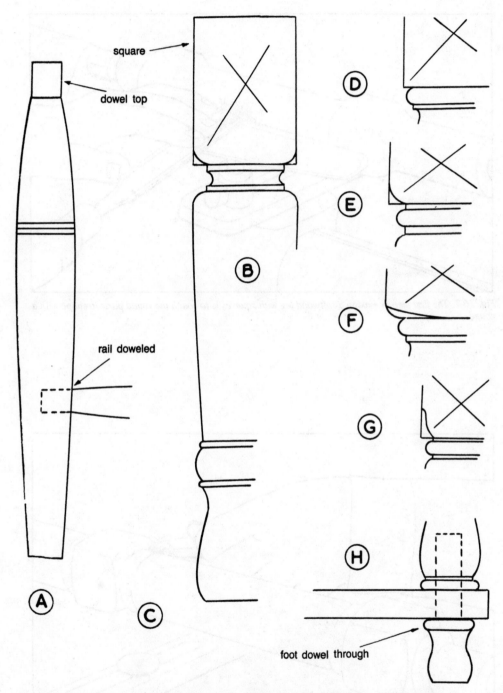

square

dowel top

rail doweled

foot dowel through

Fig. 16-1. The legs shown are intended mainly for softwood and therefore have a bold treatment.

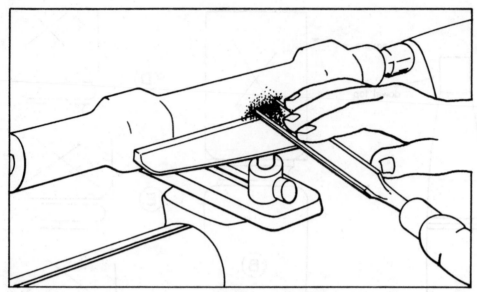

Fig. 16-2. The first step in making a softwood leg with squares is to rough the round parts to shape with a gouge.

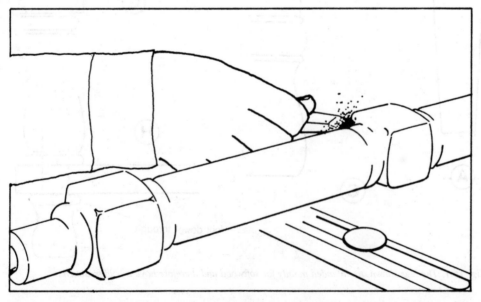

Fig. 16-3. The ends of the squares are cut and adjoining beads shaped. This leg has a dowel turned to fit into a table top.

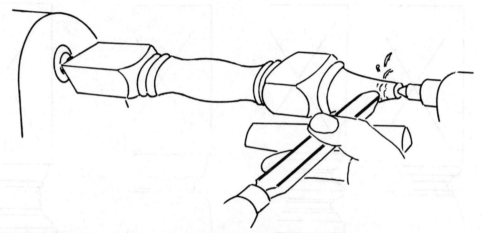

Fig. 16-4. The main part of the leg has been shaped, and the foot is being tapered.

the effect (Fig. 16-1E). This blends into a curve (Fig. 16-1F) or there can be decorative cuts at the corners (Fig. 16-1G).

A softwood leg with squares should have the round parts roughed to a circular section with a gouge (Fig. 16-2). You should tilt the tool at the ends of the cuts near the squares, so it cuts away from them and the risk of breaking away the corners is reduced. The curved ends of the squares are trued to shape with a chisel on edge, then beads adjoining the squares are shaped and the dowel top is reduced to size (Fig. 16-3). The center part is turned to shape with bold curves and no fragile detail. The foot is shaped, leaving a short length of waste at the fork center (Fig. 16-4). When the shape has been checked as satisfactory and the round parts sanded, the foot is cut off with a parting tool.

Legs in hardwood mostly have the larger part of the design toward the top (Fig. 16-5). Prominent beads and other projections should still be avoided if the table can be expected to receive knocks; they should only be included with harder close-grained woods.

Some legs on antique furniture will have squares smaller than the largest diameter turning. These can be built up, as described for bulbous legs, but where the size is not very different, the squares may be bandsawn to the reduced size and planed. If a leg is to be fitted with casters or other fittings, this should be allowed for in the overall length. It is important that a table finishes at a comfortable height for use, so the thickness of top and depth of rail should be known before planning the turned part of a leg.

Legs for lighter occasional tables are more slender than dining tables. The outlines can be generally similar, however, although care is needed not to go too deeply anywhere so as to weaken the leg (Fig. 16-6).

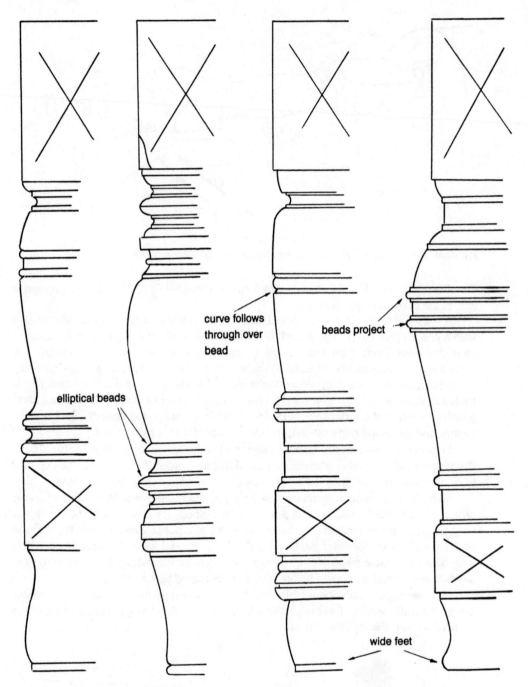

Fig 16-5. Intricate turning suitable for hardwood legs is shown.

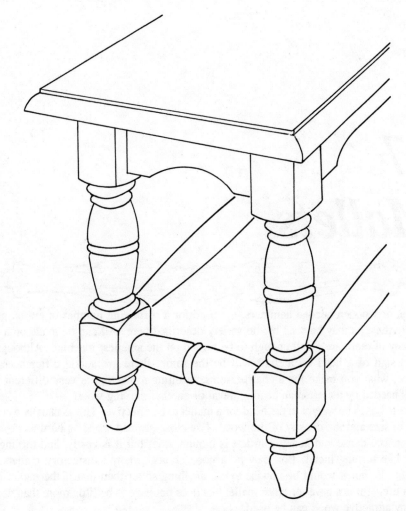

Fig. 16-6. Shown is the application of turned legs with square parts in the construction of a small table.

17
Mallets

Mallets, or wooden-headed hammers, are used for a surprising number of crafts, games and activities, as may be seen by the variety described here. All can be made on a lathe and many of them are small enough to be turned on the smallest machine. Although the basic design of a head on a shaft will be the same, there are subtle differences. For instance, what you make for a chairperson controlling a meeting is very different from what is needed by a craftsman beating metal or another carving wood.

There has to be weight in the head for a mallet to be effective. This is usually a combi-nation of size and the density of the wood. Use close-grained wood as hard as possible, and therefore dense and heavy. Hardest is lignum vitie, but it is costly, and turning it is almost like turning metal. Box may be a good choice. Many satisfactory mallets have beech heads, but it would be unwise to use anything softer than that if the mallet is for serious use. If it is a gavel or other mallet that does not have to be little more than decora-tive, any attractive wood can be used.

If the shaft or handle will be subject to much heavy use, it needs to be springy to absorb shock and resist breaking. Ash and hickory are by far the best for this purpose and should be used for any mallet that will get much heavy use. The shock transmitted to your hand is then very much less than with a more rigid wood. Whatever wood you use for a handle, its grain lines should run the full length and there should be no flaws. Knots would obviously weaken the shaft, but shakes, too, (lengthwise cracks) are best avoided.

Mallets may vary in size from dainty little ones, for some light craftwork, up to a section of three trunk on a two-handed shaft for setting paving stones. They all provide you with interesting challenges.

The head of a basic mallet (Fig. 17-1A) is a simple cylinder. Bevel or round the ends (Fig. 17-1B); this reduces or delays breaking out of the grain after prolonged use. It helps to cut a line or groove around the center (Fig. 17-1C) to locate the shaft hole. Such a plain mallet might be used for general purposes, such as driving light stakes or pegs, and is the type favored for sheet metalwork.

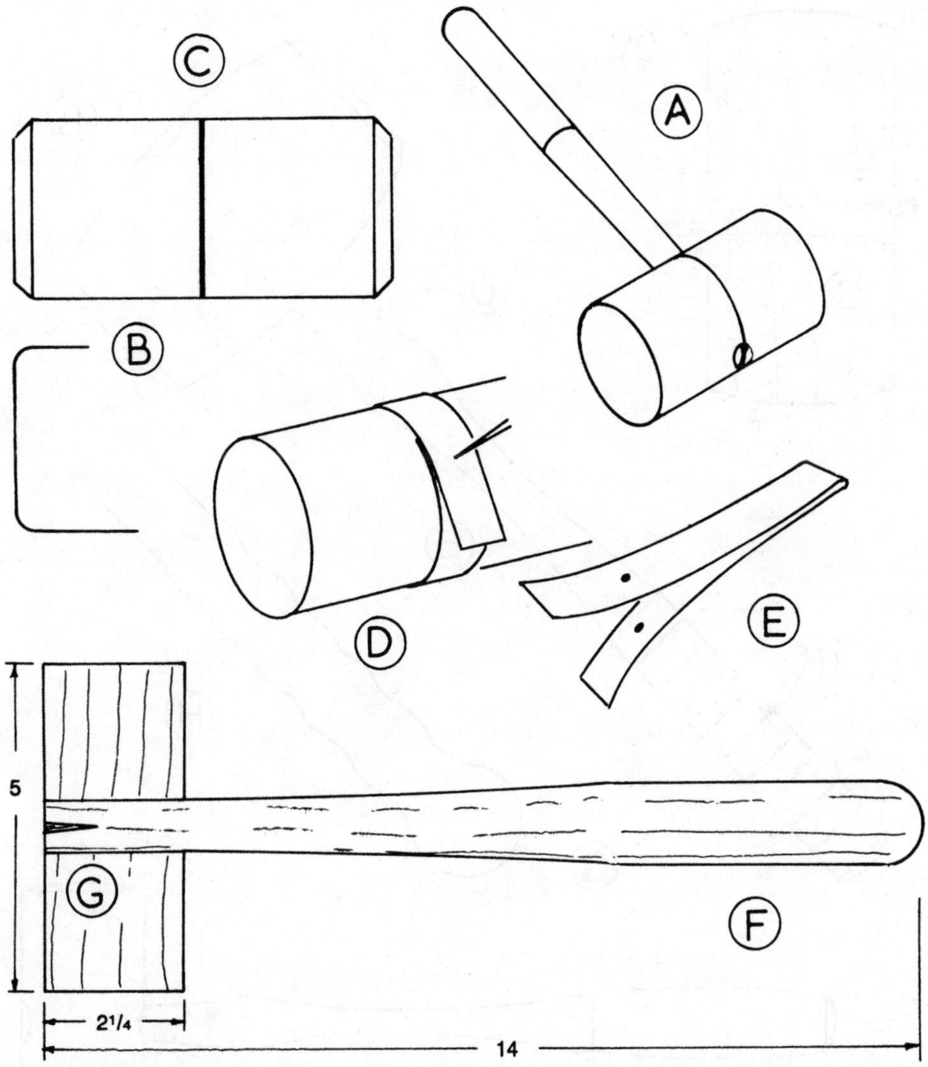

Fig. 17-1. A basic mallet design.

The hole might be $^3/_4$ inch or $^7/_8$ inch. Keep it straight if you drill from both sides. If there is a dividing head on your lathe you can locate the opposite centers easily. Otherwise, a simple way is with a strip of paper. Wrap it round and push a pin or spike through the overlap (Fig. 17-1D) at the position of the hole at one side. Open the strip and fold it so the pin holes meet (Fig. 17-1E). The fold marks halfway, so put the strip back around the mallet head and mark where the fold comes for the other center.

Turn the handle (Fig. 17-1F) a tight fit in the head hole; then, give it a gradual taper towards the grip. Experiment with holding a cylindrical strip of wood. You will probably find that no more than $1^1/_8$ inches in diameter is about right to hold. To allow for different hands, the handle end could have a slight taper away from the end. Round the extreme tip.

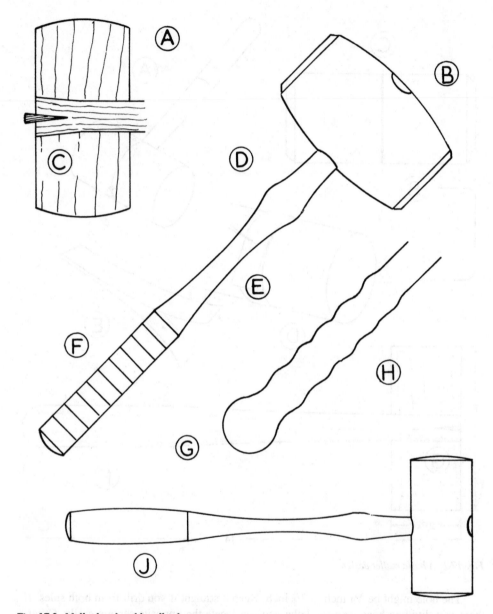

Fig. 17-2. Mallet head and handle shapes.

Put a saw cut across the end of the shaft that will go in the hole. When you assemble, have this across the grain of the head and drive in a wedge (Fig. 17-1G); then, cut the end level. Traditional mallets were assembled without glue, but you could put glue through the hole and on the wedge.

If the head loosens in use, hold the shaft without any support under the head, and hit its end. What is called a *moment of inertia* will cause the head to move further onto the shaft and the taper will provide a new grip. Re-wedge and trim the end.

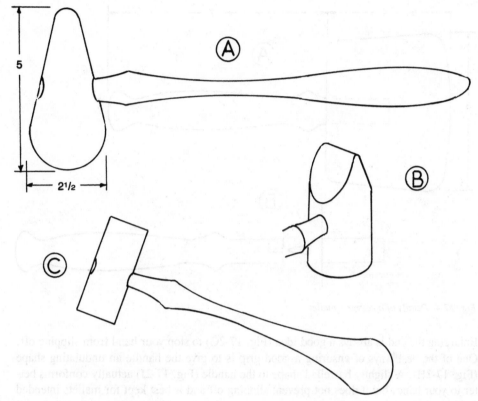

Fig. 17-3. Mallets for metalwork.

A plain parallel cylindrical head suits most purposes. There are advantages in giving the head ends a slight doming (Fig. 17-2A). This concentrates a hit at the center. It reduces wear around the circumference, where splits or splintering may occur. However, do not dome excessively, or a slightly misdirected blow may glance off.

If you want something different from a plain cylinder, remember that any cutting away of wood lightens the head, and you do not want much of that. A slight barrel shape (Fig. 17-2B) may be more pleasing. Cut a few lines around any section if you want to give it individuality.

If the head hole at the wedge side can be opened to a slight taper, the wedge will expand the shaft into it (Fig. 17-2C) and the security will be greater. Turning the taper in the lathe would be an awkward chucking problem. It is the taper at the end grain which matters and you could cut that with a gouge or round file.

Instead of a long taper on the shaft arrange a shoulder or knuckle a few inches from the head (Fig. 17-2D). This allows for a slender neck (Fig. 17-2E) to give spring where it is needed. The amount of slimming has to be a compromise between maximum springiness and the thickness needed to resist breaking.

Your hand needs a length of at least 5 inches to settle into a comfortable position on the handle. You might be able to hold a plain handle without slipping, but most will welcome an improved grip. It may be sufficient to cut lines round a plain handle (Fig. 17-2F).

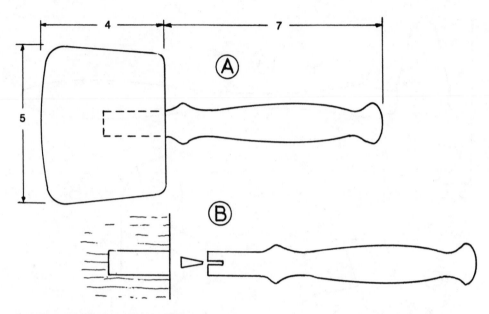

Fig. 17-4. Details of a carver's mallet.

Enlarging the end is always a good idea (Fig. 17-2G) to stop your hand from slipping off. One of the best ways of ensuring a good grip is to give the handle an undulating shape (Fig. 17-2H). A slightly barrelled shape to the handle (Fig. 17-2J) actually conforms better to your hand, but it does not prevent slipping off and is best kept for mallets intended for lighter uses.

Sheetmetal workers use a plain mallet in several sizes, as just described, and may refer to it as a *tinman's mallet*. They also use a *bossing mallet* (from "embossing") for hollowing work. This has a pear-shaped head (Fig. 17-3A) and can be made in several sizes besides that shown. So far as possible, the ends of the heads should be hemispherical.

Another sheetmetal worker's mallet may be domed or flat at one side, but the other side is something like the cross-pane of a carpenter's hammer (Fig. 17-3B). Well round the cross part. You could make more than one of these mallets with the straight edge rounded to different curves, possibly 3/8 inch and 3/4 inch in diameter.

A sheetmetal worker often uses a mallet for long periods, so spring in the shaft is important to reduce strain on the hand.

One form of light sheetmetal work is called *repoussé*. Mallets and hammers have to deliver large numbers of fairly light blows, with the handle loosely held and moving something like a ball and socket joint in the palm of the hand. The head may be small, but the shaft is slender, leading to a ball-shaped handle (Fig. 17-3C), smoothed to pivot in your palm.

The mallet favored by most woodcarvers takes a different form. Its head is cylindrical lengthwise. Plenty of weight is needed, but the handle is short. The head and the handle may be turned from one piece of wood, which may be a satisfactory method for a thin and light mallet. However, this would involve turning much wood to waste in making a large

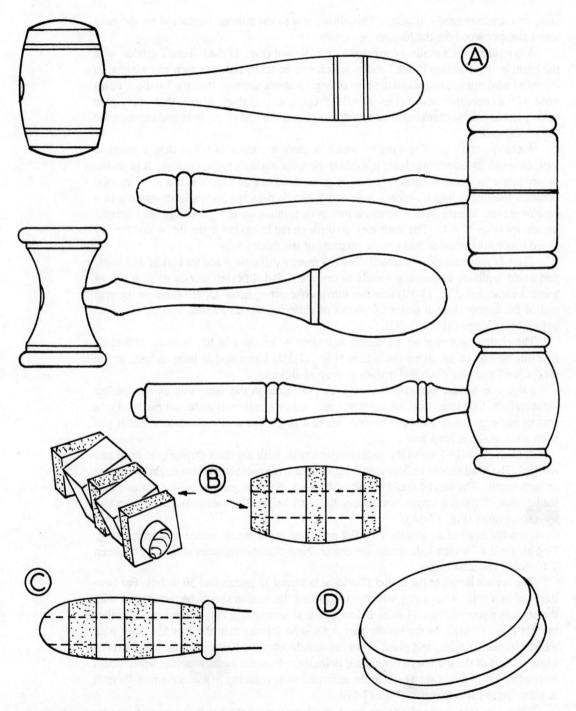

Fig. 17-5. Some designs for a chairperson's gavel.

size, so a separate handle is better. This allows you to use a dense hardwood for the head and a cheaper wood for the handle.

A typical carver's mallet of average size is shown (Fig. 17-4A). Turn the head with the grain in the direction of the handle, which can be taken right through and wedged in the usual way, but it is suggested the hole only goes about halfway, then the handle is tightened with a concealed wedge (Fig. 17-4B). Prepare a short thick wedge, then apply glue to all parts and drive them together so the wedge hits the end of the hole and expands the cut handle end.

A chairperson's gavel is a mallet which is more a symbol of office than a practical tool, although its owner may bang it hard on the table during a noisy meeting. It gives the turner scope for some decorative work. A gavel need not be big. If it has to be carried between meetings a head 2-inches long and a handle 6-inches long allows stowing in a case or pocket. You might be able to use rare or decorative wood. A few suggested designs are shown (Fig. 17-5A). The shaft may go through the head, but it should be satisfactory glued into a hole taken in about three-quarters of the thickness.

There is scope for mixing woods. Besides using a different wood for handle and head, you could laminate contrasting woods in one part. Put differing woods on a dowel of another color, and (Fig. 17-5B) turn this into an interesting head. Do the same on the grip end of the handle; turn it down for pieces of differing woods to slide and be glued on before being shaped (Fig. 17-5C).

The chairperson may not be seated at a table he or she can hit, because of a cloth covering or fear of damaging the finish. (Fig. 17-5D) Use wood at least as hard as the mallet head and glue cloth underneath to prevent slipping.

Large two-handed mallets, or mauls, can be made in the same way as the smaller plain mallets. One large type, which is not necessarily massive, is a croquet mallet. For a serious game, standard sizes are needed. Make a single one as a replacement, but if you want a set, make at least four.

A croquet mallet follows the usual construction, with the shaft through the head and wedged. The head should be heavy, so if lignum vitie is unobtainable you might use ebony or hard maple. The handle could be ash or hickory. For backyard or indoor croquet turn the handles for the full length, and reduce the mallet size. The measurements shown suit the expert game (Fig. 17-6A).

Turn the head as a cylinder with flat ends and rounding to reduce splintering (Fig. 17-6B). Drill a $7/8$-inch hole across the center. Note that the diameter should be between $2^1/2$ inches and $2^3/4$ inches.

The overall length of the mallet should be between 32 inches and 36 inches. For two-thirds of its length, it has a grip which is not turned. Its section should be rectangular with the corners removed (Fig. 17-6C). Below this it is turned in a very similar way to other mallets (Fig. 17-6D). As the handle part is finished thinner than the knuckle, start with wood $1^1/2$-inches thick, and plane down the handle after the lower part has been turned. Make the end of the shaft to fit in the head hole; then, broaden to the knuckle, which could be beaded. From this, sweep back to the unturned part, reducing to a minimum of $5/8$ inch in diameter to provide spring (Fig. 17-6E).

When you join the handle to the head, the long way of the handle section should be exactly in line with the mallet head. In the finished mallet, the octagonal handle has to be bound all over with cord or strip leather and the exposed wood should be varnished.

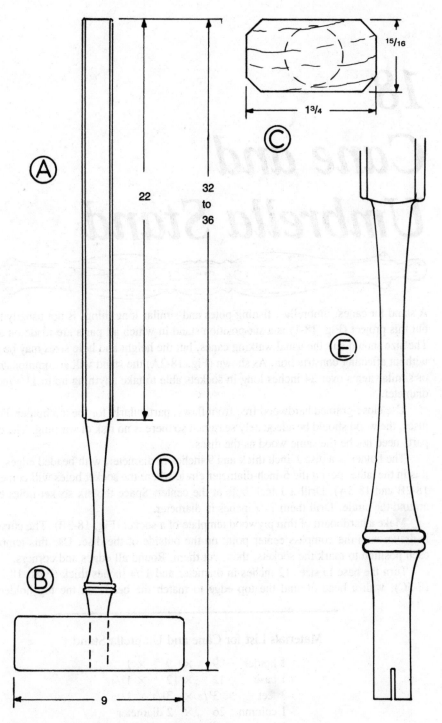

Fig. 17-6. Sizes and shapes of a croquet mallet.

18
Cane and
Umbrella Stand

A stand for canes, umbrellas, fishing poles and similar long things is not usually turned, but this project (Fig. 18-1) is a six-position stand in which all parts are made on a lathe. The size should suit the usual walking canes, but the height and hole sizes may be altered without affecting construction. As shown (Fig. 18-2A) the stand will accommodate canes or similar items over 24 inches long in sockets able to take anything up to 1¹/₄ inches in diameter.

Use close-grained hardwood free from flaws, particularly for the top holder. For both discs, the wood should be adequately seasoned so there is no risk of warping. The column parts need not be the same wood as the discs.

The holder is a disc 1-inch thick and 9 inches in diameter, with beaded edges. While it is in the lathe, pencil the 6-inch-diameter circle where the socket holes will come (Figs. 18-2B and 18-3A). Drill a 1-inch hole at the center. Space the six socket holes equally around the circle. Drill them 1¹/₄ inches in diameter.

Make a hardboard of thin plywood template of a socket (Fig. 18-3B). The curved slot is drawn with the compass center point on the outside of the disc. Use this template in each position to mark the sockets; then, cut them. Round all edges and corners.

Turn the base to size, 12 inches in diameter and 1¹/₄-inches thick (Figs. 18-2C and 18-3C), with a bead around the top edge to match the beads on the top holder (Fig.

Materials List for Cane and Umbrella Stand

1 holder	9	×	9	× 1	
1 base	12	×	12	× 1¹/₄	
3 feet	3¹/₂	×	3¹/₂	× 1¹/₂	
1 column	26	×	2 diameter		
1 knob	6	×	2 diameter		

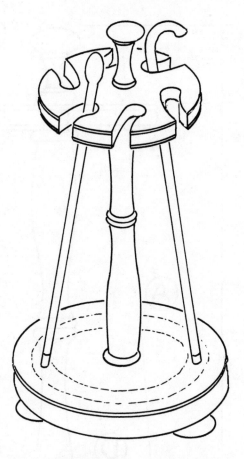

Fig. 18-1. A turned stand for canes and umbrellas.

18-3D). Turn a hollow a short distance in from the edge (Fig. 18-3E) to take the tips of canes. A groove width of about 1 inch at half the thickness of the wood should be suitable. Drill a 1-inch hole at the center.

On the underside of the base disc, space three $3/4$ inch holes for feet. Make the feet with dowels to go in the holes (Fig. 18-3F).

The column has a maximum diameter of 2 inches (Fig. 18-2D). Turn the dowels at the ends to fit the 1-inch holes in the discs. Use your own ideas for the turned design in the length, but do not reduce the diameter too much.

The knob at the top (Fig. 18-2E) may be used for lifting. Turn a $1/2$-inch dowel below the knob to go into a hole in the column dowel (Fig. 18-2F). The design of the knob may be anything you wish. When you glue the parts together, first fit the feet to the base; then, add the column. Stand this on a level surface and see that the column is upright. Add the holder and glue the knob firmly on it.

Apply a brushed finish to the completed stand. If you prefer a friction polish, apply this to individual pieces as they rotate in the lathe.

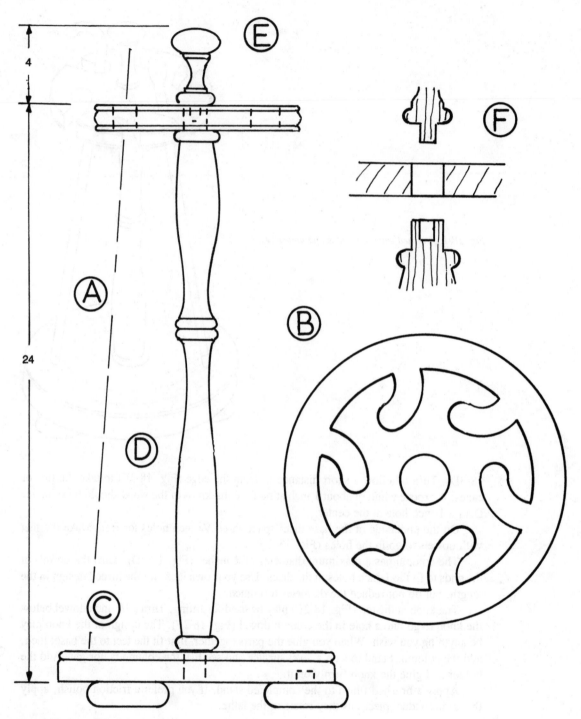

Fig. 18-2. Sizes and slot layout for the cane stand.

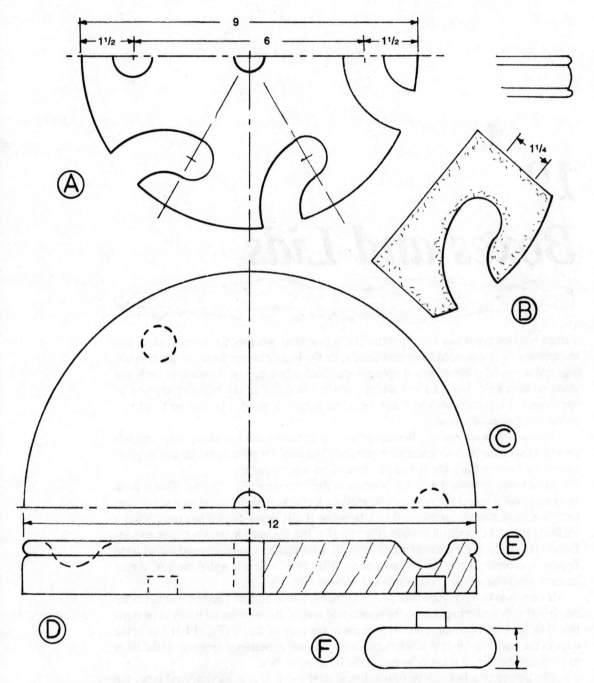

Fig. 18-3. Details of the two discs for the cane stand.

19
Boxes and Lids

Turned wooden boxes can have an attractive appearance, whether the wood is plain and the appearance is enhanced by turned details, or the beauty comes from the grain markings and the wood is turned to a simple pattern. Such a box may be complete in itself and made without a lid, but a lid will usually add to the utility of the box and improve its appearance. Lids might also be made for other things—a wooden lid can be fitted to a round metal or glass article.

The variations are endless. Besides producing attractive items, making boxes and lids provides the turner with an interesting exercise. The need for parts to match and fit gives something more to think about than just turning an artistic pattern.

Most boxes are turned with flat bottoms to their interiors (Fig. 19-1A). This is done by opening out a hole made with a bit in a tailstock chuck, with the wood on a screw center if it is small enough, or mounted on a faceplate if it is larger. Such a box usually has a basically parallel cylindrical outside (Fig. 19-1B), but the outside does not have to conform to the inside. If the contents are to be small items that have to be scooped out with the fingers, it is better to give the bottom a curve (Fig. 19-1C). If it is a shallow box, it may become more like a bowl, both inside and outside (Fig. 19-1D).

If there is to be a lid, view both parts together as a total design. The box will normally be viewed with the lid in place, so the two should match. Because the lid needs to be positioned by the way it fits, there can be a recess in the edge of the lid (Fig. 19-1E) or in the edge of the box (Fig. 19-1F). Much depends on the final appearance required. If the lid is to overhang the box, it is easier to recess the lid than the box.

The bottom of a box can be finished in several ways. If it is a cylindrical type, the method of treating the bottom should be chosen so it can be done at the same time as the box is parted off. This avoids the need to part off and then reverse the box to finish the bottom. If the section of the lip of the box is comparatively thin in section, as it usually is, there might be difficulty in chucking it without damage in the reversed direction.

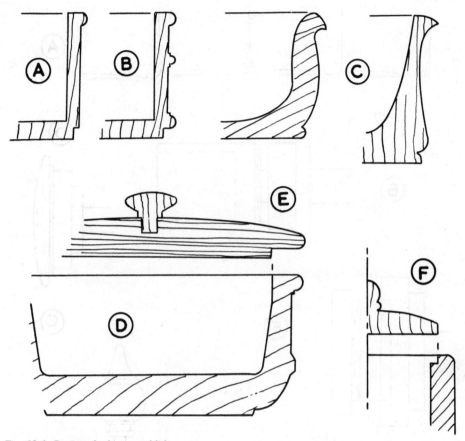

Fig. 19-1. Designs for boxes and lids.

Some possible bottom treatments are shown (Fig. 19-2A). So a box will stand level, the bottom should be turned slightly hollow (Fig. 19-2B). This can be done by tilting the parting tool or using a chisel point-downward, after cutting in with the parting tool.

If the lid is to be shallow with a knob added (Fig. 19-2C), it will usually be turned with the grain across. If the design calls for a deeper lid with the knob integral with it, the grain may be better lengthwise. Usually the bottom of the lid is kept flat and this allows fixing to a pad with glued paper, so there is no need to reverse the wood, and everything can be done in one operation (Fig. 19-2D). If the underside is to have any shaping, this should be done and the edge recessed first. It can then be pressed into a hollowed pad for the top to be turned (Fig. 19-2E).

Usually the knob will be the same wood as the rest of the lid and box, but appearance may be improved in some cases by using contrasting wood or staining the knob darker than the rest of the box. Another way of making a feature of the knob is to separate it from the lid with something of a contrasting color. This could be a metal washer (Fig. 19-2F). Plated metal gives an enhanced appearance to most woods. It could be a colored or clear plastic disc. Many plastics can be turned with wood scraping tools, so it might be possible to put a sawn disc in place; then, glue the parts together and turn the plastic to a true circle

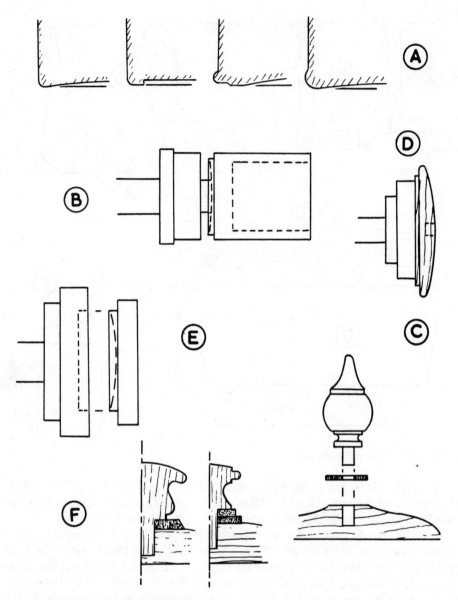

Fig. 19-2. Details of box and lid constructions.

with the wood. It is also possible to turn the knob completely in plastic. Polishing can be done in the lathe, with successively finer abrasives, followed by metal polish on a cloth. Another alternative is to buy metal knobs. If the wooden boxes are to form part of a set to stand on another piece of furniture, it may be possible to buy matching drawer and box knobs.

20
Buttons and Beads

Although the average lathe can be used for small turning as well as large turning, small items are particularly appropriate to small lathes, which do not have the capacity to make table legs and other large items. A lathe powered by an electric drill or just a small motor cannot deal with the load imposed by swinging a piece of wood of large diameter, but it may be as successful as a larger machine when used for making small items.

There is also the question of what to do with the accumulation of small scrap wood left from larger work when turning, cabinetmaking, or doing some other type of woodworking. It is possible to turn pieces of wood that most other woodworkers would regard as scrap. However, the number of odd pieces collected will be more than the turner can hope to deal with unless he has a few ideas to work on. Buttons and beads make interesting projects to turn from the smallest pieces of wood.

BUTTONS

Round wooden buttons can be quite attractive, but they have to be made in sets that match, because there are not many uses for isolated buttons, no matter how well made. If the button is to look different from a plastic button, it should have a prominent grain marking, so it is obvious that the finished button is wood. It is no use going to the trouble of making buttons on the lathe if most people look at the finished products and do not recognize them as anything more than common mass-produced buttons.

One way of making a number of buttons is to turn a cylinder to the diameter wanted. The thickness of each button can be cut in a short distance with a parting tool (Fig. 20-1A). The piece of wood is then held at the headstock end with a self-centering chuck, or by a wooden chuck made by drilling a suitable hole in a block of wood on the faceplate. The end of a button is turned. It may be simply rounded, or there can be rings cut around it (Fig. 20-1B); then, it is parted off. The surface of the next button is turned in the same way and so on until all of the buttons have been cut off.

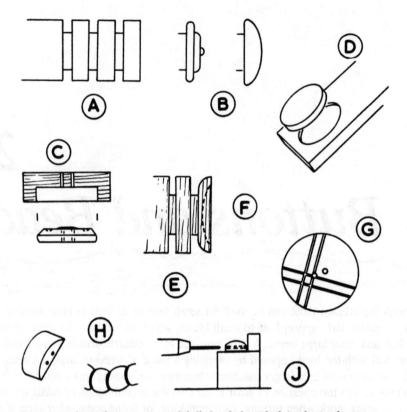

Fig. 20-1. Buttons can be made in a series and drilled with the aid of simple templates.

A button has two or four holes for thread. The best way to drill these accurately is to make a small template. Drill or turn a hollow in a piece of wood to fit easily over a button, but do not have the hollow quite as thick as the button. Drill a pattern of thread holes in this. Use it over each button in turn to drill through (Fig. 20-1C). The holes in the buttons should be very lightly countersunk to remove rough edges. This is best done by twirling a larger drill between the fingers. Using a power or hand drill might easily go too deep.

If the back of a button comes from the parting tool with a surface that is not smooth enough, it can be rubbed on a piece of abrasive paper on a flat piece of wood. It could be held against a disc sander. The problem then is holding a small button without also sanding your fingers. A hole can be made in a flat piece of wood that allows the button to stand above the surface, and this will serve as a holder (Fig. 20-1D).

Larger buttons are better made with the grain across. Usually, only a pair of these are required, and it is possible to turn them in the same way as the small end-grain buttons, with a block of sufficient thickness projecting from the chuck (Fig. 20-1E). With the larger diameter, it is possible to make the fronts hollow or with turned decoration (Fig. 20-1F).

Any of the buttons can be carved on the surface. In the simplest form, this can be lines cut across—not necessarily symmetrically—with a chisel of V-tool (Fig. 20-1G).

Buttons can be made into beads for a bracelet if fairly thick ones are trimmed with

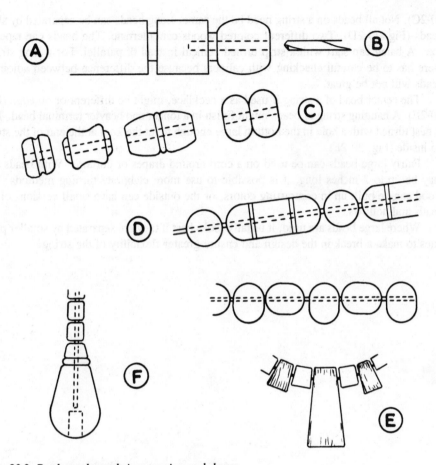

Fig. 20-2. Beads can be made in many sizes and shapes.

parallel flat sides and drilled through (Fig. 20-1H). A number of these can be threaded on elastic. Care is needed to get the holes uniformly spaced and straight through. One way is to have the drill chuck in the headstock, arrange a table, and stop over the bed at the correct height (Fig. 20-1J). If lines are drawn on the table opposite the button edges when it is in line for each of the holes, they should all finish to match.

BEADS

Make plain wooden beads in batches by turning a strip of wood between centers. Cuts with a parting tool mark the divisions (Fig. 20-2A). If a chuck is used, the wood is held by its end as the outside of the end bead is shaped. The tailstock center can support it; then, a drill is used in the tailstock drill chuck (Fig. 20-2B). This can be taken deep enough to go through several small beads. Do all of the shaping and cleaning up of the end bead while there is still enough wood to support it; then, part it off. Do the same with the next one.

These beads need not to be plain, although attractive wood shows its grain best in a simple egg shape. There can be lines cut around or the outline cut to a different form (Fig.

20-2C). Not all beads on a string need be the same. Long beads can be separated by short beads (Fig. 20-2D). Two different colored woods can alternate. The beads can taper in size. A batch can start with a strip turned conical instead of parallel. For a long string, there has to be careful checking with calipers because the difference between adjoining beads will not be great.

The center bead of a string if used as a necklace, might be different or on edge (Fig. 20-2E). A hanging string of beads might finish in a longer and heavier terminal bead. This is best turned with a hole in the bottom large enough to let the knot at the end of the string go inside (Fig. 20-2F).

Fairly large beads can be used on a cord around drapes or curtains. With beads that may be up to 2-inches long, it is possible to use more elaborate turning methods. The wood can be built up in contrasting colors, or the outside can have small versions of the beads and hollows.

Where large beads are used, it usually looks best if they are separated by smaller plain ones to make a break in the design and ensure greater flexibility of the string.

Soft-topped Stool

A stool frame might be made with turned legs and rails; then, the seat can be made by weaving cord, seagrass, leather or plastic strips. The stool may be anything from a rest for your feet or for a child to sit on, up to a tall stool for use at a bar. Construction is the same, except a tall stool needs extra lower rails for rigidity. The stool shown (Fig. 21-1) is small and a taller version would need some extra turned decoration in the legs as well as an extra set of rails.

In any stool of this type the top rails have to be at the same level, so to provide enough strength the legs must be thick enough to allow reasonable depths of holes and the rails taken in far enough to be partially mitered (Fig. 21-2A). In this way, you should get ample glue area for a good bond.

Although the lower rails could also be at the same level, it is better to change levels on a leg; then, each rail can enter further for a stronger joint (Fig. 21-2B).

It is important that a stool assembles squarely, as errors will be obvious to any viewer. This means that parts must match, particularly in lengths and the positions of holes. Slight differences in patterns may not be obvious. Note the overall proportions (Fig. 21-2C). Anything of this type looks best if length, width and height are all obviously different.

Because of the need to resist strains in joints, such as may come when a user tilts the

Materials List for Soft-topped Stool

4 legs	15 × 1³/₄ diameter
2 top rails	15 × 1 diameter
2 top rails	11 × 1 diameter
2 bottom rails	16 × 1¹/₄ diameter
2 bottom rails	12 × 1¹/₄ diameter

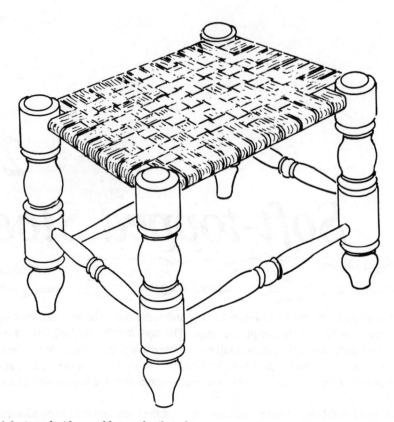

Fig. 21-1. A stool with turned legs and rails and a woven top.

stool onto two legs, use close-grained hardwood for the legs. Use the same wood for all parts. The rails should be straight-grained.

When you make the legs (Fig. 21-3A), start with one and use it as a pattern for the others, or use a marked strip of wood to get features in the same places. Use calipers to check that legs are the same diameter, particularly at joint positions.

Making the top rails thicker at the center (Fig. 21-3B) counteracts any tendency for the finished stool top to look, or actually be, hollow on the edges. Aim at a good fit in the leg holes by testing ends with a hole of the same size in scrap wood.

The lower rails (Fig. 21-3C) have to be the same lengths between leg surfaces as the top rails, but allow for them penetrating a little further. Make sure decorations are symmetrical by using a marked strip of wood as a gauge.

Mark and drill the holes in the legs carefully. Pair the drilled legs, because of the difference in the lower rail levels.

Assemble opposite long sides first. Glue the top rails in as far as they will go, after cutting miters on their ends. Avoid clamping by securing with fine nails driven from inside (Fig. 21-2D). The lower rails provide adjustment. Glue them in as you move the legs in or out at the bottom to get them parallel (Fig. 21-2E). Drive fine nails here as well. Check flatness and squareness, and see that the second side matches the first.

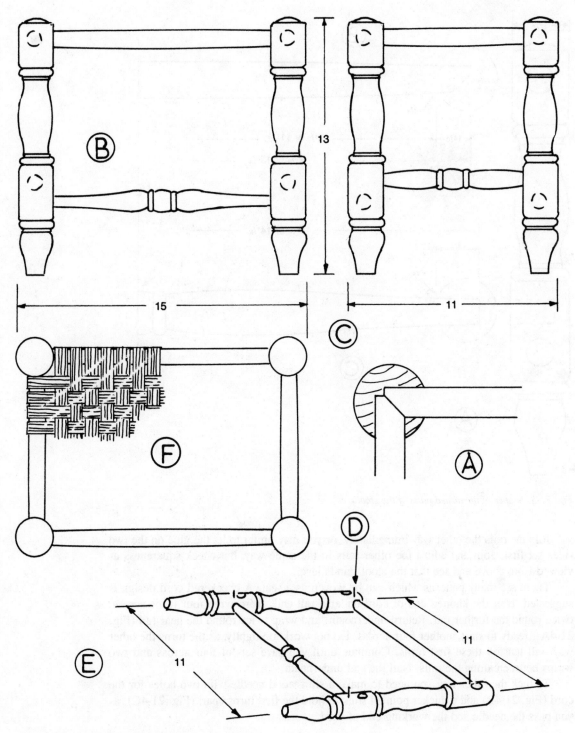

Fig. 21-2. Sizes and layout of the soft-topped stool.

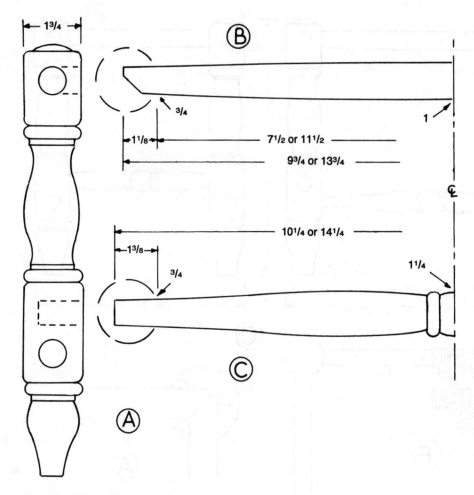

Fig. 21-3. Shapes of the turned parts of the stool.

Join the rails the other way immediately, or you may prefer to let the glue on the two sides set first. Join and adjust the other rails in the same way, but check squareness as viewed from above and see that the stool stands level.

There are many patterns which can be woven as a seat. A checkered cord design is suggested. Nail the knotted end of cord under a rail end; then, wrap four turns across, twice round the further rail. Return underneath, and wrap twice round the near rail (Fig. 21-4A), ready to start another four across. Do not work too tightly, as the turns the other way will tension these first turns. Continue until you have sets of four across and two wraps between along the rails. Nail the end underneath.

To tuck the other way you need to make a slim wood needle with two holes for the cord (Fig. 21-4B) and a thicker pointed stick to hold the first turns apart (Fig. 21-4C), as you pass the needle and the working end of cord.

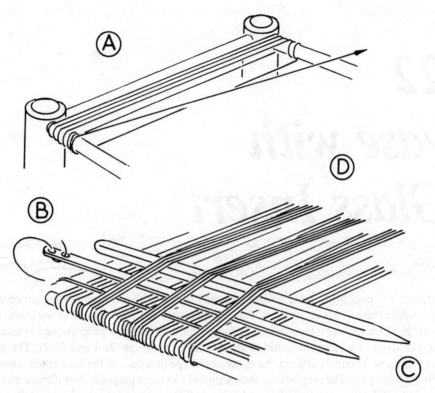

Fig. 21-4. Starting weaving cord on the stool top and using a wood spike and needle to start working a checker pattern.

Wrap in a similar sequence in this direction with four across and two wraps between, going over and under alternately to make a checker pattern on top (Figs. 2-2F and 21-4D). Underneath, you may merely return straight across, or work a pattern of large squares there. Press the turns tightly along the rails, and use the pointed stick to pull the crossings straight and square.

22
Vase with
Glass Insert

Although it is possible to make a wood vase and treat it with a waterproof sealant or varnish inside, there is always the risk that this may fail and allow water to soak into the wood. It is better to use a glass insert. In this example, the vase is proportioned to take an insert of about 1³/₈ inches in diameter and 4-inches long (Figs. 22-1 and 22-2). The vase is in two parts. The two parts may be of the same type of wood, or the base could contrast with the other part. The proportions shown should suit most purposes, but if there may be a large floral display, a wider base could be turned. If you want to make the vase taller, the base diameter should be increased.

Turn the base on a screw center or faceplate. It might also be made by drilling a wood disc and mounting it on a mandrel between lathe centers. This method allows a large base to be turned hollow underneath, so that it should stand more firmly. Keep the surface that has to be in contact with the upper part flat. There are, however, other possible edge designs that could be turned instead of the one that is shown.

The hole of the glass insert is the important process in the upper part. Carefully center the wood and drill it for the insert. Use either a drill press or a drill chuck in the lathe tailstock. Make it an easy fit and allow for about a ¹/₄ inch of the glass to project above the finished vase, so that it can be gripped and pulled out. Turn a plug with a slight taper to push into the end of the hole and project a short distance with its own center dot. Mount the wood between centers with the plugged end towards the tailstock. Turn the dowel end by checking the size with calipers, or reverse the wood so that the spur center drives the plug while you turn and check the dowel at the other end, with the actual hole in the base as a gauge.

Glue the parts together and put a disc of cloth under the base.

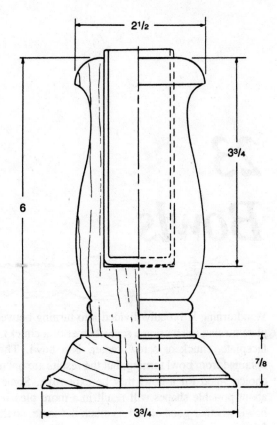

Fig. 22-1. *Suggested size and shape for a vase to take a glass insert.*

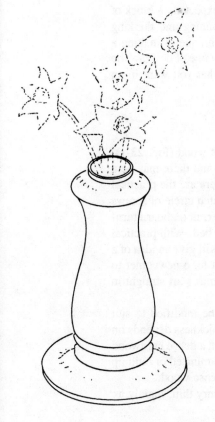

Fig. 22-2. *Vase with a glass insert; this is made from two pieces of wood with the grain of the base across.*

23
Bowls

Woodturning is broadly divided into turning between centers (spindle turning) and faceplate turning (also using a screw center or a chuck). The most popular project turned on a faceplate, chuck or screw center, is a bowl. There is considerable satisfaction to be obtained from bowl turning, but the results are not always as good as expected. A block of choice wood for a bowl may be expensive. Some time spent in planning and thinking about possible shapes will result in a more pleasing design. The technique of making a bowl, whether good or bad, is much the same, so the problem is really one of design. The following notes and illustrations are offered as a guide to getting what you want in an attractive form, from your block of wood.

DESIGN

The design of a bowl starts with the size of the available block of wood (Fig. 23-1). After the circle has been sawn, the general proportions can be seen, and there may be a case for a preliminary sketch of what is to be made (Fig. 23-2A). There are the practical problems connected with the method of mounting in the lathe. The pitch circle of screws through a faceplate may limit the size of a base. If the lathe does not permit outboard turning, the possible maximum diameter is limited by clearance above the bed. With practical considerations taken care of, a few experiments with freehand curves will give an idea of a possible outline. The finished bowl may not be exactly that shape, but for a newcomer to bowl turning, the sketch is a starting point. Anyone with experience may start straight in with a gouge and work to a shape which is being visualized.

Some possible shapes are shown in Fig. 23-2B. Curves might be modified to suit larger diameters (Fig. 23-2C) or thicker blocks (Fig. 23-2D). Bowl thickness depends on the wood. There must be clearance over the points of fixing screws, but a dense hardwood can be taken thinner than a lighter wood (Fig. 23-2E). If the blank is laminated or built up from blocks in any way, it is inadvisable to go as thin as with solid dense wood.

Actually, thinness is a relative thing. Some turners make bowls very thin, mainly as

Fig. 23-1. A tray, a deeper bowl, and a small bowl showing the effect of simple curved sections.

an expression of skill, but apart from risks of breakage in use, a thin shell may warp and twist due to taking up and giving off moisture from the air. It is better to have most of the bowl thick enough to give stability, but the edge may be thinned (Fig. 23-2F). This gives a delicate appearance as the thicker lower part is not obvious.

CURVES

It is possible to make a bowl to almost any curve and get an acceptable result. The tightness of the curve should vary. If it closes toward the top, the popular turned-in shape results (Fig. 23-3A). If the curve is less near the bottom, the bowl will have better capacity (Fig. 23-3B) for things like piled-up fruit. For a complete break from the more enclosing bowl, the section can go out almost conically, but it is unwise, from a design point of view, to have straight lines in the section. It looks better for everything to be curved—even if only very slightly (Fig. 23-3C).

Most wooden bowls in normal use are viewed from above, possibly at about 45 degrees, but unless the bowl is put on a high shelf, its profile is not usually the main feature. What is seen is the inside and a short distance down the outside from the lip; this should be kept in mind when turning these curves. Obviously, the shape should be pleasing all over, but if the rim area—inside and out—has poor shaping, the whole bowl fails.

The base of most broad bowls is rarely seen. Consequently, a simple small projection is all that is needed (Fig. 23-3D). This also suits mounting, because there is no need to turn the bowl over to work on the base. However, there may be designs where a recess below is needed; this can be turned first and the block mounted on a turned pad. If a bowl is broad in relation to the size of its base, it may be advisable to turn a recess to take a lead block (Fig. 23-3E) to provide stability. This would also be advisable if the base is high or the bowl is more like a cup in its proportions.

Almost any pattern can be turned on a base if it is to be a feature. In general, it looks better if its top is narrower than its bottom (Fig. 23-3F). That is also more stable than the less attractive narrower bottom (Fig. 23-3G). If there is not much depth in the base, a fairly plain outline (Fig. 23-3H) is better than one turned with many flourishes.

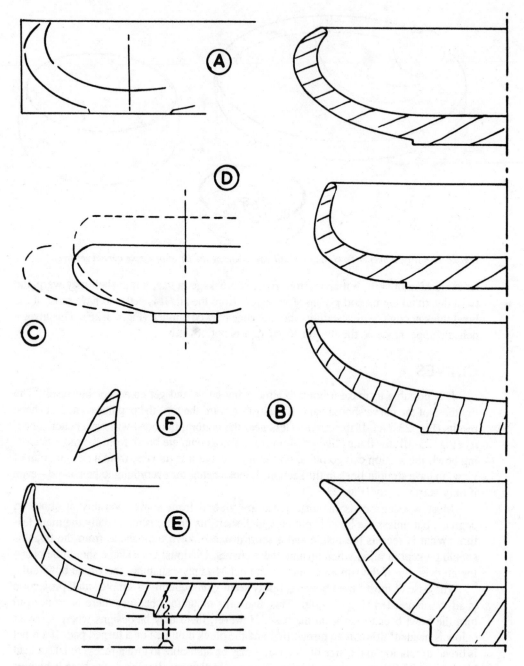

Fig. 23-2. Suggestions for various bowl outlines.

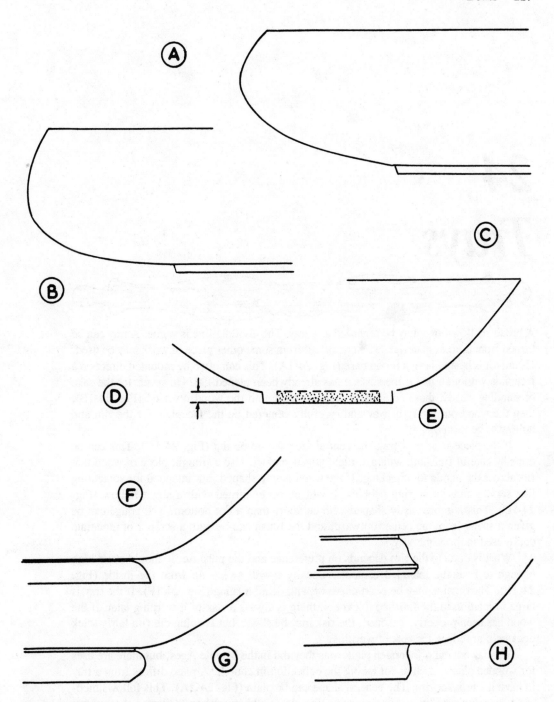

Fig. 23-3. Suggestions for relating the base to a bowl.

24

Trays

A broad shallow bowl may be regarded as a tray. The dividing line is vague. A tray can be turned from thinner material so that an offcut from some other piece of work may be used. Usually it is best to have a broad base (Fig. 24-1A). This can often be mounted direct on a faceplate without a pad if the surface has already been planed flat. However, for the sake of standing steady, there could be a recess turned with the wood reversed (Fig. 24-1B), then the wood put the right way and carefully centered on the faceplate for the rim and hollow to be turned.

If the piece is to be a tray, the central area should be flat (Fig. 24-1C). This can be done by careful finishing with a straight-edged scraper. Use a straight piece of wood that fits across the inside for checking. If the wood is tray-shaped, but intended for something like serving nuts or sorting pebbles, it will be better turned with a slight hollow (Fig. 24-1D). This is more easily shaped with certainty than a flat bottom. The gouge can be given a swing from the center outward, and the finish can be with a scraper of moderate curve used in the same way.

What is done to the rim depends on preference and the purpose. It should stand high enough to hold the intended contents. Usually it will sweep up from the inside (Fig. 24-1E). The outside may be plain curve or with detail turning (Fig. 24-1F). If the tray is large in relation to the finished thickness, there is always a risk of it warping later. If the wood has been properly seasoned, the risk may be slight, but keeping the rim fairly thick does help to reduce the risk of warping.

We may not eat off wooden platters as they did in the Middle Ages, but there are uses for wooden plates, such as for taking the collection in church. A plate differs from a tray in having a broader rim. The general shape can be plain (Fig. 24-2A). This follows modern trends, but a traditional or a reproduction plate will have elaborate turning, both above and below the rim (Fig. 24-2B). How the inside is treated depends on the use, but for coins and similar objects, it helps to turn a shallow recess for a piece of leather or plastic (Fig. 24-2C).

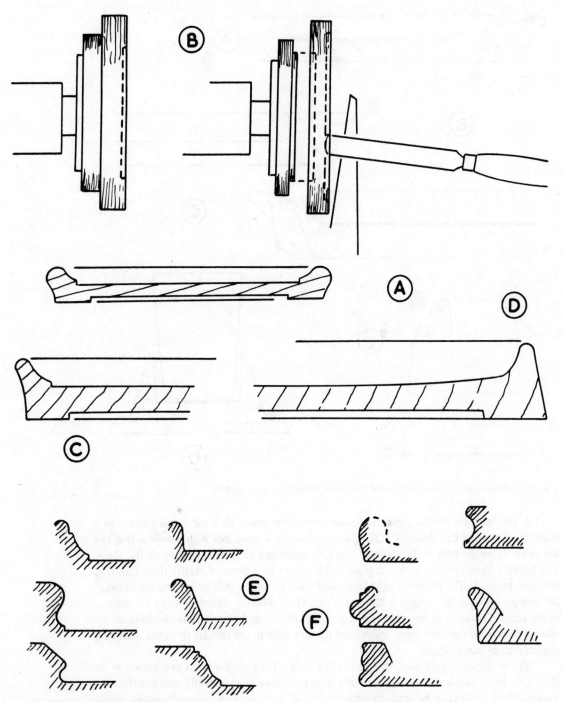

Fig. 24-1. Patterns for large plates or trays.

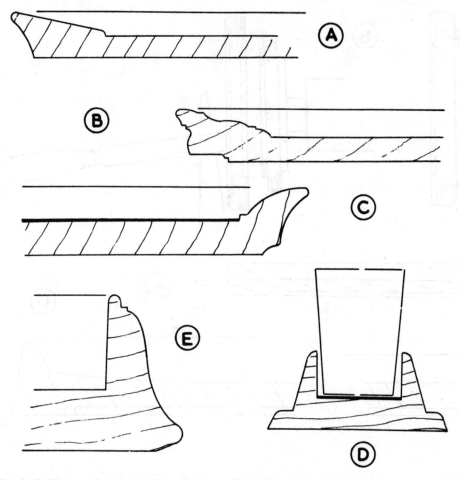

Fig. 24-2. Plates can be turned with broad rims used for making glass stands.

A similar form can be used to provide something better than the usual coaster as a stand for a glass or cup (Fig. 24-2D). The shape is like a plate, but with a hollow that is a very easy fit on the base of the glass. It is not intended that the stand should grip the glass. The inside can be covered with soft plastic. Thin cork or a piece of plastic floor covering can also be used. The outside might be turned with a molded outline toward the bottom, but leave a space to get fingers under for lifting (Fig. 24-2E). There is scope for a great many outside patterns to be made. Even in a set, there can be variations. So long as the overall dimensions are the same, individual treatments will not detract from the matching appearance of many stands.

Similar stands can be made for use in the shop. They do not need decoration to do their job, but a nicely-made article always inspires better workmanship and gratifies the maker. These stands can be made to support cans of glue, varnish, or anything else liable to be knocked over. They benefit from being tightly fit so their broad bases provide steadi-

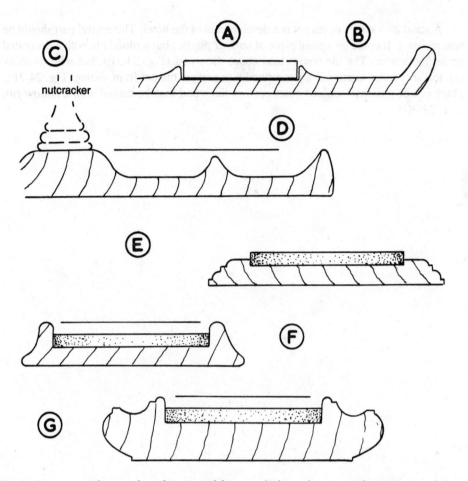

Fig. 24-3. A tray can be turned to take a central feature, which may be a nutcracker or a piece of tile.

ness. Small trays and bowls are also useful for nails and tacks. A curved inside makes it easier to scoop out the contents than trying to pick nails, screws, or other objects from rectangular boxes.

Not every bowl or tray is a simple container with a smooth interior. There may be a tile in the bottom. There are also other things that can be inset. A circular box of cheese sections may be accommodated in a recess with a lip around it, and the outer part available for crackers (Fig. 24-3A). A circular tile in a raised center of a tray will become a cheese platter. The same idea can be used with a taller container. The rim then serves to catch crumbs or as somewhere to put a spoon (Fig. 24-3B).

There are some nutcracker fittings to mount on a base. One of these could be located on a raised center in a bowl (Fig. 24-3C). A further refinement is to turn the inside of a broad bowl with a division, so uncracked nuts are in the outer part and broken shells fall into the inner part (Fig. 24-3D).

A stand for a coffee or tea pot is a development of the bowl. The central part should be heat resistant. It could be a plain piece of cork or plastic, but a round tile with a decorated center looks neat. The tile could stand above the wood (Fig. 24-3E), but with its shiny surface, it is better to provide a rim around it to prevent the pot from sliding (Fig. 24-3F). There can be a narrow molded outer edge or the wood may be turned with a hollow rim (Fig. 24-3G).

Index

Index

Other Bestsellers of Related Interest

24 ROUTER PROJECTS—Percy W. Blandford

Percy Blandford, whose step-by-step guides to woodworking and metalworking techniques have become standards in their fields, has now compiled a truly unique collection of 24 exciting projects made with a standard router including boxes, tables, stools, shelves amd more. 128 pages, 81 illustrations. Book No. 9062, $6.95 paperback only

THE WOODWORKER'S ILLUSTRATED BENCHTOP REFERENCE—William P. Spence and L. Duane Griffiths

Whatever your woodworking question, you'll find the answer in this book, and what's more, you'll find it quickly and easily. Specifically aimed at the homecraftsman, *The Woodworker's Illustrated Benchtop Reference* covers every facet of woodworking, from choosing the right wood to bringing up a luster on your finished projects. Nearly 500 pages and more than 600 illustrations present the latest woodworking materials and technology, time-proven techniques, expert insight, and classic woodworking projects. 496 pages, 657 illustrations. Book No. 3177, $24.95 paperback, $34.95 hardcover

FENCES, DECKS AND OTHER BACKYARD PROJECTS—2nd Edition—Dan Ramsey

Do-it-yourself—design, build, and landscape fences and other outdoor structures. The most complete guide available for choosing, installing, and properly maintaining every kind of fence imaginable. Plus, there are how-to's for a variety of outdoor structures, from sheds and decks to greenhouses and gazebos. Easy-to-follow instructions, work-in-progress diagrams, tables, and hundreds of illustrations. 304 pages, illustrated. Book No. 2778, $14.95 paperback only

BACKYARD BUILDER'S BONANZA
—Percy W. Blandford

In this book, master woodworker Percy Blandford provides woodworking projects that will help you create an outdoor living space ideal for relaxing or entertaining. Decks, doors and gates, safety and privacy fences, chairs, lounges, tables, benches, pergolas, brick walkways, and more are among the 52 step-by-step plans presented in this book. 210 pages, illustrated. Book No. 3174, $10.95 paperback, $17.95 hardcover

77 ONE-WEEKEND WOODWORKING PROJECTS—Percy W. Blandford

Let this guide put the fun back into your hobby! Overflowing with step-by-step instructions, easy-to-follow illustrations, dimensioned drawings, and material lists, this indispensable guide includes plans for 77 projects: tables, racks and shelves, take-down book rack, low bookcase, corner shelves, magazine rack, portable magazine bin, shoe rack, vase stand, beds and cabinets, yard and garden projects, toys, games and puzzles, tools, and more. 304 pages, 226 illustrations. Book No. 2774, $18.95 paperback only

THE WOODWORKER'S SHOP: 100 Projects to Enhance Your Workspace—Percy W. Blandford

Making tools, accessories, and equipment for the home workshop, that will stay in the workshop, is the focus of this new book. More than 100 projects are presented in all, each with step-by-step instructions, detailed drawings, and materials lists. Ranging in complexity to suit any degree of skill, all are designed to help you do your work faster, more economically, and with greater accuracy. 270 pages, 174 illustrations. Book No. 3134, 14.95 paperback, $22.95 hardcover

101 OUTSTANDING WOODEN TOY AND CHILDREN'S FURNITURE PROJECTS
—Wayne L. Kadar

Turn inexpensive materials into fun and functional toys. Challenge and charm the youngsters in your life with building blocks, pull toys, shape puzzles, stilts, trains, trucks, boats, planes, dolls and more. This step-by-step guide is abundantly illustrated and provides complete materials lists. 304 pages, 329 illustrations. Book No. 3058, $15.95 paperback, $24.95 hardcover

CLOCK MAKING FOR THE WOODWORKER
—Wayne Louis Kadar

This collection of easy-to-build clock projects contains everything you need to create beautiful, hand-crafted wooden clocks. Here's your chance to construct a pendulum wall clock, butcher block clock, barnwood clock, clocks you'll be proud to give as gifts, clocks you'll want for your own home . . . over 50 in all! Best of all, *you can build them at low cost!* 192 pages, 297 illustrations. Book No. 1648, 14.95 paperback only

THE PORTABLE ROUTER BOOK
—R.J. De Cristoforo

If you've always thought of your portable router as a pretty unexciting tool, capable of little more than producing decorative edges on certain types of woodworking projects . . . then this book is just what you need to start taking advantage of all the creative possibilities that the router can really offer! Plus, you'll find how-to's for making your own router stands, jigs, fixtures and guides for use in creating such special effects as fluting, reeding, tapering, and peripheral cutting. 368 pages, 466 illustrations. Book No. 2869, $14.95 paperback, $24.95 hardcover

THE TABLE SAW BOOK—R.J. De Cristoforo
"R.J. De Cristoforo is the outstanding tool authority in the world." —*Popular Science*

This book is a complete and practical approach to basic and advanced table saw functions. Detailed instructions and hundreds of illustrations are included for crosscuts, rips, miters, tapers, chamfers, dadoes, compound angles, and more. 352 pages, 500 illustrations. Book No. 2789, $16.95 paperback, $23.95 hardcover

THE JIGSAW/SCROLL SAW BOOK, with 80 Patterns—R.J. De Cristoforo
". . . the outstanding tool authority in the world." —*Popular Science Magazine*

R.J. De Cristoforo's in-depth presentation of this multifaceted tool makes it clear that the scroll saw's capabilities are extensive. In addition to the 80 patterns featured in this book, project plans for making a scroll-saw stand, a hinged draftsman seat, and a blade storage unit are included. 304 pages, 375 illustrations. Book No. 3269, $18.95 paperback, $27.95 hardcover

MAKING MOVABLE WOODEN TOYS
—Alan and Gill Bridgewater

This book contains 20 toy projects that will challenge and excite the creative woodworker in you. From Russian nesting dolls to an American folk art baby rattle, traditional pull-along toys to English soldiers, these are the toys adults enjoy making and children enjoy playing with! The designs employ whittling and lathe work among other techniques. Precise, over-the-shoulder instructions and numerous work-in-progress illustrations guide you through every step of construction. 240 pages, 106 illustrations. Book No. 3079, $14.95 paperback, $23.95 hardcover

MORE PROJECTS FROM PINE: 33 New Plans for the Beginning Woodworker—James A. Jacobson

Make beautiful and functional gifts from pine—for your home, for your friends, for profit! This easy-to-follow guide offers 33 more woodworking projects . . . each requiring only a small investment of time and money. Detailed drawings and photographs make this the perfect resource for the novice woodworker, yet the material lends itself to skillful variations at all levels. Success with the simpler projects will give you the confidence to move on to the more advanced pieces. 192 pages, 131 illustrations. Book No. 2971, $10.95 paperback only

WOODWORKING TECHNIQUES, TIPS, AND PROJECTS FROM A MASTER CRAFTSMAN
—B. William Bigelow

Here's where the woodworker who's acquired basic skills can begin to grow as a craftsman, learning many specialized techniques for using the table saw, the band saw, the wood lathe, the router, and the drill press. Bigelow has chosen an outstanding collection of 25 projects to illustrate each of the techniques he presents. Complete with detailed plans, step-by-step photographs, illustrations of finished pieces, and a listing of tool and material suppliers. 240 pages, 237 illustrations. Book No. 3255, $16.95 paperback, $26.95 hardcover

Look for These and Other TAB Books at Your Local Bookstore

To Order Call Toll Free 1-800-822-8158
(in PA and AK call 717-794-2191)

or write to TAB BOOKS, Blue Ridge Summit, PA 17294-0840.

Title	Product No.	Quantity	Price

Subtotal $ _____

☐ Check or money order made payable to TAB BOOKS

Charge my ☐ VISA ☐ MasterCard ☐ American Express

Acct. No. _____ Exp. _____

Signature: _____

Name: _____

Address: _____

City: _____

State: _____ Zip: _____

Prices Subject to Change Without Notice.

Postage and Handling
($3.00 in U.S., $5.00 outside U.S.) $ _____

Please add appropriate local
and state sales tax $ _____

TOTAL $ _____

TAB BOOKS catalog free with purchase; otherwise send $1.00 in check or money order and receive $1.00 credit on your next purchase.

Orders outside U.S. must pay with international money order in U.S. dollars.

TAB Guarantee: If for any reason you are not satisfied with the book(s) you order, simply return it (them) within 15 days and receive a full refund. **BC**